Making Peace with
Our Own Death

Tom Owen-Towle

W0010460

Flaming Chalice

P R E S S

Flaming Chalice Press™
3303 Second Ave.
San Diego, CA 92103
Tel: (619) 933-1121
Website: www.tomo-t.com

10 9 8 7 6 5 4 3 2 1
First English Edition 2021

ISBN 13: 978-0-578-87547-7

Library of Congress Catalog Card Number: 2020925960

Cover and book design by CenterPointe Media
www.CenterPointeMedia.com

Cover Painting by Millard Owen Sheets (1907-1989)

Dedication

The beloved shall grow old, go ill, and be taken away finally.
No matter how tenderly we love, how bitterly we argue,
how cunningly we hide, this is what shall happen.
—MARY OLIVER

One of us will go first, my beloved
    if it is I, please convey to any gathered grieving
        a portion of what and who I tried to resemble
        and if it is you
  don't blush or dare shush me
      let the world receive an earful of your feats
      and my undying fondness

Making Peace with Our Own Death

Table of Contents

Foreword

Owen-Towle's text is a prayer to push away the fear we often
associate with the end of life. It's a call to move "tenderly . . .
homeward," without using up our remaining energy on
being afraid of the shadow death often casts.
—Rev. Nancy McDonald Ladd

The Catholic Church I grew up in didn't have a choir of robed angels singing songs of heavenly praise. I don't remember an organ or
even a piano under the peeling blue paint of that sanctuary, though
there must have been one. Instead, our music came almost exclu-
sively from a nerdy Sunday school teacher named Mr. Scheller,
who was friends with my dad. He had a guitar and a stool to sit on,
and occasionally a lady with a tambourine would accompany him.
He sat just to the left of the pulpit and sang flowing hymns written
in the 70's as a part of the post-Vatican II move toward contempo-

rary worship. Mr. Scheller donned a monumental moustache and wore pleated pants. He poured forth his whole heart, singing about eagle's wings and God's love extending to the ends of the earth.

Truth be told, my sister and I really liked to make fun of Mr. Scheller. We would do bombastic imitations of him in the parking lot after mass. Get a beer or two in us and we'll do that same impression still. And yet, for all of our carefully cultivated teenage detachment, we also sang those sweet 70's tunes with full-throated joy.

Years later, after I had lovingly left the Catholic Church and woven my way into the Unitarian Universalist ministry in which I now serve, I found myself with young clergy from all around the country. We were gen-Xers in the early stages of our careers, wondering just what it was we were embarking on, while our congregations changed and sometimes crumbled around us.

At the first meeting of this collective, I walked into the retreat center and was greeted by a colleague who thrust a bible in my hand and asked if I would share one of the readings for vespers that night. I said "yes," but I was afraid. In the chapel at the appointed time, I fumbled with the onionskin pages, nervous that somehow this Unitarian Universalist newbie would bungle or "out" myself for the non-believer I thought I was.

Even now, I don't remember what scripture I read in the chapel that night. What I do remember is what came next. Sitting silently, without even a guitar to carry the tune, my new colleagues started to sing. I had not heard the hymn since I was a child. "Be not afraid," they called out plaintively. "I go before you always. Come, follow me, and I will give you rest." The words flowed over me. I knew them all by heart. Of course, it was one of Mr. Scheller's sweet hits, written in 1975 by Catholic songwriter Bob Dufford. It's a song I'd mocked and laughed about and sung throughout the course of my adolescence, and there I was, at the beginning of a career in Unitarian Universalist ministry, crying my way through it, feeling blessed by every note.

"Be not afraid," we sang. And for that moment, I wasn't afraid.

"I go before you always, come follow me," we sang. And for that moment, I didn't feel alone.

"And I will give you rest," we sang. And for that moment, peace felt possible.

As I sat reading my colleague Tom Owen-Towle's deeply pastoral and profoundly moving reflections in his latest book, that song came back to me all over again. His volume is a hymn in prose, reminding us of those same reflections I learned as a child, passed through the clarifying and challenging lens of our Unitarian Universalist faith.

He teaches the age-old lessons of courage, companionship, and trust in ways that are linked to time and history but examined anew through the theology of our progressive tradition. Owen-Towle's book is a supremely personal, practical, and pastoral resource in facing our own mortality.

Be Not Afraid

There is a passage in Rev. Tom's book that takes the reader on a pilgrimage to the Memorial Garden at the First Unitarian Universalist Church of San Diego, where the author served so ably, for twenty-four years, as co-minister with his life-mate, Carolyn. In that bucolic place dropped smack dab in the middle of the most beautiful piece of land imaginable, Tom recounts the way that they would orient new members to the Church. The Owen-Towles would walk out to that Memorial Garden and introduce them to the ones who came before, each named on a plaque to mark their enduring impact on the congregation and the world.

Reverends Tom and Carolyn were inviting all new members to meet the people who built this place. See the names of those who still dwell as a cloud of witnesses. Recall the ones who spent evenings in board rooms and long afternoons teaching children how to think and pray and hope and survive. Meet the cranky and gentle ones, the irascible but tenacious folks who built this parish. It's not an institution you join, but a lineage. That was the essential orientation of new members in their congregation, and it is the orientation Owen-Towle invites readers to share through his guidebook on making peace with our own death.

As we contemplate the last quarter or so of our lives, we too must understand that we belong to a long and storied lineage. And if, in fact, the generations to come will count us among the cloud of witnesses, we need not fear mortality. Owen-Towle's text is a prayer to push away the fear we often associate with the end of life. It's a call to move "tenderly...homeward," without using up our remaining energy on being afraid of the shadow death often casts.

Surely, this instructive and inspirational book reaches us during a time when we collectively dwell in the shadow of death. With the Covid-19 pandemic still raging, I write this *Foreword* shortly after officiating at the online memorial service of the eldest member of our congregation. He was 98 years old. He had served in half-a-dozen presidential administrations during those years but spent fully half of his years on this earth as a dedicated member of a single congregation ... the very Bethesda, Maryland community I am so proud to serve today.

I was afraid to lead his service during these unusual times. I thought the center could not possibly hold under such circumstances.

And yet, I came away grateful for the ministry that rises above all the fear, including my own. Even online, we can make a pilgrimage to the sacred places. Even then, we can bear witness to the ones who brought us so far by faith and foibles and great effort. Even in the valley of the shadow of death, the shape of a life well-lived is clear and evident.

Whyever should we be afraid?

I Go Before You Always, Come Follow Me

Tom is clear that the purpose of his book is to ensure "that our final laps on earth be meaningful ones." He applies the lessons of science, psychology, social justice, poetry, and art to that central task. But he is also a theologian—which means that this text cannot achieve its purpose without contending meaningfully with the relationship between God and all of us messy, wonderful human beings.

Even for those among us who harbor something of an on-again-off-again relationship with the divine—even for those of us who are pretty darn sure there isn't a *there there* in the supernatural sense—the theological task of meaning-making remains essential in both our living and our dying. In order to receive grace, one must make peace with the idea that grace comes from somewhere. In order to gain acceptance of what is, including the reality of death, one must make peace with the truth that there is much we cannot control.

As Tom so beautifully puts it—"the cornerstone of progressive theology is evolution." Thus, our belief systems can and must evolve right up to our final moments.

Part of how we make meaning in later life is to acknowledge that there are always new insights beyond what we have previously debated, articulated, or imagined. Finding that ever-changing meaning requires a level of engagement with the holy that takes us out of our own egos and into relationship with that which is larger than ourselves. This relationship does not have to be one of submission. It's not based on anybody's idea of doctrinal correctness. Rather, it's what comes when we trust the Eternal to keep on making meaning alongside us . . . in and through it all, up to our very last day.

Owen-Towle invites us to move through life as an unceasing divine-human partnership in which we co-collaborators learn to trust each other in ways that are both vulnerable and sustaining. After all, trust has always been more reliable than "belief." Trust is something you can depend on. It's founded in a relationship. We lead, and we follow. Meaning-making happens in a grand collaboration until, ultimately, we lean back into the mystery and trust that the Eternal will hold all.

And I Will Give You Rest

Tom is a colleague's colleague, retired after serving 50+ years of long and loving ministry in relationship to both his parishes and his friends. He's found bold and joy-filled avenues for his creative spirit during what he calls "re-firement" and uses this book to point the way for others to do the same.

When Owen-Towle writes of the pandemic, he writes with heartbreak, but also with a measure of peace that is grounded in the later stage of life that both blesses and challenges him. Rev. Tom shares sorrow, but also deep gratitude, for the long days that stretch out as well as the generosity of empty, quiet time.

In contrast, I am a 40-something mother of two young children. Those two young children have been out of in-person school for almost a year. That is the story of the pandemic in my life. In varying degrees, I also have the blessed responsibility of attending to four pets, one spouse, 500 congregants and a fair amount of my own unresolved anxieties. My life is not restful in these days. I am in the busy time—the life stage often associated with long hours and little sleep. When I think of rest, it is hard to think past the dream of a single afternoon to myself with a good book and a cup of tea. What I want is cessation of the constant whirl, though I know that there will come a day when I look back upon midlife and bless every beautiful thing that came alongside it.

Tom's book invites us to seek and find calmness in our living no matter what life stage we may be muddling through. Yet the rest that he invites us to, especially near end of life, isn't the isolating and anodyne "rest" that is so often presented as a kind of euphemism for death. Anodyne euphemisms for death are the very kind of thing Tom Owen-Towle dislikes the most. Let us not talk of "passing away" or "eternal rest," when what we are really talking about is the stark and beautiful wonder that is death itself. Let us not navigate broad emotional perimeters around and over and underneath the truth of our mortality, rather let us face it with a gaze of blessing and a willingness to be lovingly shaped by it in the affairs of our daily living.

The deep and abiding serenity Owen-Towle articulates on these pages is born not from an avoidance of death, but from a deep engagement with all of its trials and wonders. He helps us learn to plan and dream and grieve and grow right until our final breath. This is an eminently "practical" volume. And, always, both personal and pastoral.

At midlife, I yearn for the rest of silence to escape the pressures of all this living. In later life, Rev. Tom points the way toward a deeper rest that keeps us engaged in living. Both are real and beautiful.

As you read this gift from Tom Owen-Towle's own heart, I know you will find yourself, as blessed as I am, by the transformative ministry in evidence on each and every page.

Be not afraid. You do not go alone. Learn to lead and learn to follow. And the pursuit of peace will be your final adventure.

With gratitude,
The Rev. Nancy McDonald Ladd
author, *After the Good News: Progressive Faith Beyond Optimism*

CHAPTER ONE

Reflecting Upon Death
Amidst a Pandemic

Dying is the last thing I'll have
a chance to do well.
I hope to hell I can.
—LAEL WERTENBAKER

FRIDAY THE 13TH OF MARCH, 2020

We are dwelling smack dab in the midst of an escalating corona-virus pandemic that's devastating our globe. We are driven inside, washing hands and drinking bottles of water, storing up on toilet paper, food supplies, sanitary wipes, gloves and masks, staying home as safely and securely as possible, and practicing the problematic art of entwining without entangling our lives.

And we're valiantly trying to stay awake in the here-and-now.

It's crucial to look *back*, burying regrets or relinquishing dreams and to look *ahead* in hopeful anticipation, but life can be lived only by looking *around* in the eternal now. Charlie Brown quipped: "Someday we will die!" And Snoopy replies: "Yeah, but every other day, we're alive!" Wakeful folks honor that truth, even during a pandemic.

My chosen faith, Unitarian Universalism, is a hard-hat and deep-seat religion, claiming that the holy dwells in the details. It beckons us to handle every encounter or event as a sacrament. Celebrate life, here and now, not months away or far off in some heavenly realm. Or as my college basketball coach kept driving home during practices and games: "Hey guys, all you've got to do is win the next play, win the next play!" Easier said than done, especially during our 21-game losing streak!

The Hebrew Scriptures remind us: "This is the day that the Lord hath made; rejoice and be glad in it." It may be your final day, so cherish it. Note that *rejoice* is an intransitive verb that requires no object, meaning that we are primed to take pure delight in existence itself. May our souls never harden to the marvelous, or as the Pennsylvania Dutch say: "May life wonder me!"

Even now.

We would do well to synchronize our life-flow with the poem, *Pandemic*, by Unitarian Universalist ministerial colleague Lynn Ungar, a verse which has gone viral:

What if you thought of it
as the Jews consider the Sabbath—

the most sacred of times?
Cease from travel.
Cease from buying and selling.
Give up, just for now,
on trying to make the world
different than it is.

Sing. Pray. Touch only those
to whom you commit your life.
Center down.
And when your body has become still,
reach out with your heart.
Know that we are connected
in ways that are terrifying and beautiful.
(You could hardly deny it now.)

Know that our lives
are in one another's hands.
(Surely, that has come clear.)

Do not reach out your hands.
Reach out your heart.
Reach out your words.
Reach out all the tendrils
of compassion that move, invisibly,
where we cannot touch.

Promise this world your love—
for better or for worse,

in sickness and in health,
so long as we all shall live.

Ungar's message is poignantly relevant during this time of "self-quarantining:" urging us to cancel outside activities while refusing to cancel our loving and being loved. We're summoned to pursue, more intensely than ever, our favorite solitary arts such as singing and doodling, decorating and renovating our abode, gardening and texting, cooking up a storm of enticing recipes, cautiously communing with intimates, and extending our affection to animals and plants, near and far.

One key virtue for weathering COVID-19 is flexibility, elasticity, or hardiness. Charles Darwin (1809-1882), an evolutionary naturalist of immense contribution, emerged from a non-conformist Unitarian background. His claim was that survival comes not from the strongest and most intelligent beings but from the most supple, adaptable, and resilient among us. This is sage counsel during this surging contagion, as we must be prepared to adjust our current plans and future hopes.

Several times a year, over the past decade plus, I've offered lectures and held discussion groups in senior living communities on conscious aging. I focus each session on a distinct spiritual lesson for staying vital. During COVID-19, I've had to adapt to zooming with my elder cohorts in their retirement facilities, a fresh and tricky assignment for this non-techie.

Although it's a markedly different world for all of us, there have been some delightful discoveries or periodic "refreshings," to use the picturesque Quaker term. We're finding novel ways of savoring life while being cooped up, aren't we? During this time of compulsory "slowth," we're developing indoor rituals and activities that are most fulfilling. We're tackling more intricate jigsaw puzzles, reviving long-forgotten arts such as painting or stitchery, returning to a childhood musical instrument, performing an overdue clean-up of our closets, and compiling scrapbooks of photos and articles for future generations.

Gunilla Norris, meditation teacher and psychotherapist, deftly phrases the nourishment found in such moments of disciplined Sabbath:

These little stops bring something of ourselves back to the whole, the way a bee brings nectar to its hive . . . the pauses add up.

Sabbath signals a way of traversing space and time that includes outbreaks of song and delight, restorative siestas and rituals, contemplation and conversation. Yes, "the pauses add up." The scriptures of every religion remind us that the Sabbath is given to us and created for us, not the other way around. That's a handy reminder, for Sabbath-time loses pertinence and power if it becomes another batch of compulsions, untrue to one's heart.

COVID-19 offers the opportunity to grab pint-sized Sabbaths, wherein we can breathe, smile, relax, and meander. It is the season to dally and dawdle more, travel outside-in, take the temperature of our souls, and pare life down to basics.

Slow-poking and confined, we're finding ingenious ways to "stay in touch" with loved ones, even build new friendships, from a distance. We are meditating more consistently than before. We are listening pensively to music. Some are journaling for the first time or memorizing pieces of scripture and poetry, then repeating them out loud as fortifying mantras. Folks are revisiting neglected volumes on their bookshelves for a boost. We're eating more slowly, masticating every morsel and saying explicit thank yous to those laborers who produced, harvested, and prepared our food, from plants to animals to people. In sum, we are fashioning original, as well as recovering ancient, spiritual practices to stay stimulated and mindful.

During this raging pandemic we are granted (especially, elders who fortunately don't have to earn a living!) increasing opportunities simply to be playful—by ourselves, with others, and alongside our favorite animals.

Remember: we were created to stomp and holler, chortle and dance, just for the hell of it, as well as the health of it. We're here on earth, among other things, to play for play's sake, not to play with a why in mind, or with an opponent, or with a finish line, but just to play, because we're *homo ludens*—playful, silly, fun-loving creatures—luxuriating in what Sarah McCarthy calls "our own liberating ludicrousness and practicing being harmlessly deviant." We disregard this existential condition at great peril both to ourselves and to the cosmos itself, especially as we age and roll toward our *finis*.

And we're also finding rest too—more mid-day naps than usual. There are places in our every day, in our very home, in our soul itself, where we can find refuge from life's relentless swirl and whiplashes. We need to know, find, and visit said places of solace and sanctuary on a regular basis. One tip: check out the animals and plants in your region; they spend the majority of their time . . .

slumbering. Nature's rhythm is worth emulating. Before we rest in final peace, we're summoned to live in peace . . . daily.

The pandemic is also forcing us into the relatively foreign state of mystery, hour by hour. The Greek word *mys* in the word mystery means shutting the eyes or mouth, because mystery has the power to overcome and its essence is omnipresent. Therefore, in engaging mystery, we are often driven to silence, muteness, and dumbness, compelled to shut-up, no easy or comfortable feat for loquacious, logical types. But dwelling amidst some mystery every day prepares us for our entrance, upon death, into the residence of ultimate Mystery.

My wife, Carolyn, has long-practiced a family-honored custom called "entering the silence." When she needs to be tranquil and undisturbed, like her mother and grandmother, Carolyn alerts all those nearby: "I love you, and I am entering the silence: a realm of sealed lips, closed eyes, and unruffled soul. In my own time, and not before, I will return to be with you." This going apart has been a well-used discipline of religious sages throughout the millennia. What a propitious practice to pursue during COVID-19.

I'm a slow learner, but, as my days dwindle down, I'm acknowledging silence to be a substance not a vacuum. Silence exists. It is a presence rather than an absence, especially when nighttime arrives. In the monastic tradition, they call the time from dusk to dawn the "Great Silence."

Between the last evening recreation and first morning meditation one is obliged to be quiet. I've gone on Catholic guided retreats and know this Sabbath firsthand. Nancy Wood (1936-2013) reveres the Great Silence with this blessing:

It is our quiet time,
we do not speak,
because the voices
are within us.
We rest with all nature.

Great Silence: great with growth of soul, great with slumber composed of respite and stirring, and great with demons of the dark. Great also because in our dreams the gods and goddesses are more likely to visit us, knowing humans to be defenseless, at home, purged of ego, and unoccupied.

Befriending the Great Silence is a worthy vow during our "twilight" time. As elders and crones, we are petitioned to explore its consecrated, albeit, terrifying hollows, and entertain its favors. Furthermore, we need to feel equally comfortable entering the Great Silence with or without loved ones by our side. Because one day, when we cross over into our final silence—absolute darkness and stillness—we want to be spiritually seasoned.

Ready or not, more spiritual benefits arise during COVID-19. We're reacquainting ourselves with the supreme discipline of all: conscious breathing. Breathing is the bridge from body to mind. It builds up the lungs, strengthens the blood, and revitalizes every organ in the body. The curious thing about breathing is that it can be evaluated both as a voluntary *and* an involuntary action. I am doing it, yet it is happening to me. Breathing is an activity destined for self-sustenance, but it also constitutes our main link with all existence, for the same air flows in and out of the lungs of every living thing. It is both ordinary and transcendent. Breathing is truly a religious act, wherein our individual spirits partake of the Infinite Spirit.

The regular practice of conscious breathing has proven to reduce stress, blood pressure, and cholesterol levels. A Harvard study discovered that nursing home patients, in their eighties and above, were given instruction in group meditation. The residents felt more cheerful, functioned better, and, on the whole, lived longer than non-meditators.

I launch every morn by intoning, for several minutes, some version of the mantra of Thich Nhat Hanh:

In, out . . . deep, slow . . . calm, ease . . . smile, release.
Present, moment . . . wonderful, moment.

Or I chant, Sarah Dan Jones' *Meditation on Breathing* (#1009 in our *Singing the Living Tradition* hymnal): "When I breathe in, I breathe in peace. When I breathe out, I breathe out love."

However, conscious breathing isn't just a self-nourishing endeavor. *Tonglen* is the Tibetan Buddhist practice where we intentionally breathe in suffering and breathe out comfort, benefiting ourselves and all sentient beings, since torment is a universal condition. *Tonglen* enables us to embrace human anguish: take it in, and then transform it. *Tonglen* is a most fruitful endeavor to practice during COVID-19 . . . both for ourselves and for other earthlings. It embodies empathy.

Myriad elders have prayed and chanted, danced and sung, studied and meditated, perhaps visited a sacred site or been on a holy pilgrimage, but often during the twilight of life, we arrive at the realization that there's nothing nearer the hub of spiritual contentment than paying attention to our own breathing in and breathing out.

Breathing is our best and closest friend. Having every one of the 75 trillion cells in our bodies breathing more slowly and harmoniously is decisive to a hale and holy zenith.

Staying apart, staying connected should be our goal during this pandemic. Physical distancing dare not diminish our emotional connectivity. Paul, in the Christian Scriptures, invites people to address one another as "yokefellows." He urges us to treat one another in a respectful and collaborative fashion. We are solitary creatures, to be sure, but change the *t* to a *d*, and we are also solidary beings. One of the keenest songs in our hymnal is the short but compelling #402: "From you I receive, to you I give, together we share, and from this we live." Our human fates are inextricably hitched. We are kin. We are yokefellows.

When members of the Blackfoot tribe greet each other, they do not say, "How are you?" but rather "How are the connections?" recognizing that all earthly existence (virtual *and* actual) comprises an interwoven network of bonds . . . each one influencing the other. Or as the Zulu phrase, *ubuntu*, in African discourse, signifies: "a person is a person because of other people." We do nothing entirely on our own. *Me* is always subordinate to *we*. You and I, while not in the same boat, are definitely paddling in the same ocean. Actually, the concept of *ubuntu* goes beyond human beings to include all species, every living entity. We are wholly interconnected. May we observe such wisdom throughout and beyond this pandemic.

We are never too old, too weak, or too late to comfort our fellow creatures. Our body grows weary and will wear out; yet, time exists and challenges present for seniors to be well-doers: to bake some bread, trim a bush, make a COVID-19 mask, adopt a stray animal, or send a note . . . and when such endeavors become too strenuous, then we can smile, wail, laugh, reminisce, or hum.

We should never feel above or beyond the recipient of another's touch and concern. We dwell on earth to comfort *and* be comforted. I'll never forget our grandmother, Clorinda Ramirez Towle, who lived with us the last 20 years of her life, after her husband shockingly committed suicide. "Clorie," as we nicknamed her, became increasingly arthritic and debilitated, until the day she pulled my brother and me aside and said:

Well, my darlings, my hands don't work much anymore. They can't knit or play cards; they certainly can't cook and even have trouble holding silverware.

Remember, when I held you little guys on my lap and would sing to you Spanish ballads? Well, Philip and Tommy, I'm going to need you two youngsters to assist me more and more, okay? I'm going to need your hands to hold mine. And please, promise that you will sing sometimes with me.

I'm going to need your comfort.

Undoubtedly, one of the reasons I ended up becoming a pastoral caregiver and my brother Phil became a social worker/therapist was this early training in our own house.

During the close of workshop sessions of *Mindful Dying*, I convene a caring circle and share a ritual that was introduced to me by Unitarian Universalist fellow traveler, Billie Barbara Masten:

Please gather together in a circle and grasp hands for a moment . . . then drop both hands to your side. Now extend your right hand forward, view your palm, and see therein your special power and gifts as a human being. Then clasp it to your chest and own your strength.

Drop that hand and tender your left hand which, upon viewing, reminds you of your weaknesses and shortcomings as a creature. Now, pull that hand to your torso and internalize your weaknesses.

Drop your left hand; then rejoin hands as a whole group.

I invite you to recognize that your strength is holding the weakness of your neighbor and your weakness is being held by another's strength. Together, hand in hand, strengths and weaknesses intertwined, we will create and sustain the caring community.

May it come to pass.

Then we leave for home . . . fortified as yokefellows, today, tomorrow, forever.

During my eleventh hour, I'm choosing to give birth to a volume on homestretch living-and-dying well. Hopefully, this personal, philosophical, and eminently practical handbook—*Making Peace with Our Own Death*—will resonate with other elders and the younger generations too, fellow pastors and curious laity alike. It will be my final missive of love.

To be sure, many of my cherished activities are negated for

the time being: singing in nursing homes (I grieve, thinking of those who may have died by the next time I'm able to show up!); volunteering at the homeless center; mentoring youth, up close and personal; traveling for pleasure or professional purpose; and watching my San Diego Padres live at Petco Park. Moreover, my weekend workshop in Tucson, Arizona in early April has just been postponed. The topic: *Mindful Dying.*

One week ago, I conducted a memorial for a woman, a professional nutritionist who was known to take great care of her own self as well as the rest of us. Our friend's death sent searing shockwaves through her relational web, especially elders and crones, many of whom wisely chose not to attend the service. This vibrant 73-year-old succumbed, during the night, to a major heart attack. Our funeral service was the last public event held in the First UU Church of San Diego sanctuary, since gatherings of 250 (now 50 going towards 10) and above were discouraged by state and local health officials in California.

One of my early spiritual mentors in ministry was Betty Baker whose compassionate perspective squares with mine:

My concept of ministry is companioning: walking hand in hand with our parishioners and others in joy and sorrow . . . being truly present in each relationship.

Well, COVID-19 thwarts caring professionals from "walking hand in hand," so we must companion one another in imaginative ways. We are withstanding a heartbreaking season when folks are unable to visit or say full and satisfactory goodbyes to loved ones who are suffering and/or dying. Survivors are burdened with additional grief, remorse, and unfinished conversations. This pandemic has robbed us of considerable human agency.

The time has arrived when memorial services are being conducted online. A zoom funeral won't do any of us full justice, but we'll manage what we must to pay final homage to each precious creation. But, deplorably, during COVID-19, more socially, racially, and economically marginalized folks than usual will die, lost in the cracks, void of satisfactory commemoration. We would remember them in our thoughts and prayers.

Prayer is "deep calling unto deep," as the Psalmist puts it. When we pray, we are doing something seemingly impossible. We are talking to somebody who's actually not somebody else, but as near to us as our heartbeat. We discover the Eternal One as a spirit deep within us—a nudge, a comfort, and a co-conspirator of sorts. The word for praying in Hebrew is *hitpael* and resides in the reflexive voice. It connotes self-assessment, wherein humans inwardly examine ourselves before we beseech Yahweh for support. Praying then becomes a collaborative effort. It enables us to be accompanied, to proceed "unalone."

Prayer invariably commands our own human sweat and effort, whether we're a child, mid-lifer, or an elder. In fact, sometimes prayer and action are synonymous. In our Unitarian Universalist worship, we frequently say: "And may service be our prayer." I imagine that's what the 19th century social reformer and abolitionist Frederick Douglass meant when he said: "I prayed for twenty years but received no answer until I prayed with my legs." I know that I personally never felt more empowered than when I was praying-marching as a 23-year-old Bay Area seminary neophyte for racial equality . . . from Selma to Montgomery, Alabama, back in 1965.

The Latin root for the word prayer is *precarious*, which reminds us that the genuine article remains an uncertain, even shaky, adventure. Does prayer work? Yes and no. Sometimes, a person recovers, even from a life-threatening illness, and, sometimes, not. Prayer is precarious, just like all the whole shebang.

Therefore, as I face my own death or companion others doing likewise, I don't pray for a result so much as for resolve and calm even when healing is unlikely, and for abundant love within, among, and beyond us. And my best praying is short and sweet. Long prayers tend to telegraph neediness or arrogance. Praying, whether alone or with others, isn't the time to get fussy about words. It's not the time to impress humans or overwhelm God with extraneous information. All that's important is that we're totally truthful and trusting.

We Unitarian Universalists believe in lovingly holding people in our thoughts and prayers. We light candles and offer chants on behalf of sisters and brothers. We affirm that human souls radiate comforting energy.

I'm not talking about superstition or magic, but prayer as an act by which we place another's burden or being in the center of our consciousness.

This morning I'm holding all my nursing home cronies in my prayerful embrace. During the COVID-19 lockdown, I don't get to sing among them. Their health is so fragile, both caregivers and residents alike, especially now. God, how I miss them! I can only cradle them in my prayers.

Of course, prayer may or may not change reality, but it does change both those who are praying and those being prayed about. Of that I'm pastorally sure. Prayer keeps the gift of love flowing, and love keeps the heart open and human bonds animated, which is the best we can do.

The pandemic is mushrooming across the world and might, after a brief decline, reemerge this Fall, so say the scientists. Indeed, it may become "the new normal" the remainder of each and every senior's sojourn. Like most home-stretchers, Carolyn and I luckily don't have to worry about returning to full-time work or negotiating childcare and school duties. We weep for the youngers struggling to make ends meet and maintain domestic civility. Our daily life continues to be shaped by choices rather than by duties, and for that, Carolyn and I are truly thankful.

As one well-situated in a state of what I smilingly call "re-fire-ment," I'm most alive when my heart's "on fire" and when there's ample "fire in my belly." I require juice and passion to stay resourceful. I carry an identity card in my wallet that states my name with contact information. The word *Merrymaker* is emblazoned at the top followed by my main re-firement joys: Ministry, Music, Magic, and Marriage.

Hence, I'm signed on as a ministerial veteran, occasionally on duty, zooming or otherwise. And my beloved Carolyn, what occupies her days? Among other pursuits, she is still donning her own ministerial robe, calling and connecting deeply with friends and family—expressly, folks who are forlorn or forgotten.

My life-mate and I are talking and walking more. Thoreau reminds us that the *saunterer* is one who strolls in measured manner, with one eye on nature, the other on soul—treating the terrain and all therein, as sacred. Only, in our case, we're wearing gloves, visors, and masks.

We're also wholeheartedly backing the "UU the Vote" project as well as "Vote Forward" . . . nudging folks to participate in America's sacred right and patriotic responsibility of casting a ballot. Now, in mid-October, we just mailed 650 epistles at our local post office. Nothing noble—we're just trying to serve our homeland while staying at home. Today, we learned that one of our cherished colleagues, Judy Welles, was writing similar letters the very day she died. Now, *that's* heroic devotion to country!

And, yes, we're crooning favorite ballads together, holding hands firmly, viewing again treasured family videos and documentaries (such as the Ken Burn's 2001 PBS miniseries on "Jazz"), and kissing delicately. But not all is sweetness and light. Due to tight-quarters and constant closeness, we're bickering more. Testiness can lead to nastiness. We apologize and move on. After 47 years of marriage, we've learned one foremost lesson: love means accepting one another's frailties and appreciating one another's graces. Love means being supremely present, considerate, and forgiving.

Partnership, at its richest, is for marathoners not sprinters. I like the way Spanish diplomat and writer, Salvador de Madraiga (1886-1978), put it: "Love me little by little, be not in haste. For I would have you love me long. Love me slowly, love me deeply, love me long." True love requires the kind of commitment that assumes a future where things might get better or worse, but our loving will endure.

Blessedly, folks are performing ingenious forms of heart-to-heart resuscitation. A fellow-UU, whose life has been interwoven with ours for over two decades, just called. She is doing precisely what Rev. Ungar urged: "Do not reach out your hands. Reach out your heart. Reach out your words." Our friend knows that caring and kindness are contagious, too.

All our live-long days, needs for companionship yearn to be met through appropriate and affectionate touch, comforting touch. However, during this global pandemic, we've pretty much had to trade physical for emotional touch. Although our sense of touch fades as we age, our heart and skin hungers persist. Touch is one of our last pleasures to relinquish.

There remain innumerable ways to touch and be touched. If we live alone, we can learn to enjoy the one we're with, namely, ourselves. We can massage our own body, relishing a kinship often underdeveloped. Gladys rubs and hugs a little kitten, named *Green Eyes,* who wanders over from the apartment next door, every day or so. Touching and being touched by a cat delivers physical connection and nourishment for our friend during her homestretch.

And then there is "staying in touch" in another sense of the word. More emails and calls are arriving, one from our dear daughter-in-law offering to assist us in any way possible. Another person ordered one of my books on self-care, so she would be, as she put it, "occupied with some uplifting reading." And then my distant cousin e-mailed me, and a comrade of five-plus decades from Davenport, Iowa, composed a note saying she couldn't physically write anymore. This would be her final letter to us; but it won't be ours to her.

And surprise of surprises, we just got a phone call from Helmut and Monika Baum in Germany, folks from whom we have not heard in a dozen or so years . . . straightway, across the ocean, from their hearth to ours.

On and on the run the soulful links we humanoids are forging. You know what I'm referring to, because a similar thing is likely transpiring in your own domicile. Despite being housebound, we are still connecting. E. M. Forster starts one of his novels thusly: "Only connect . . . and the isolation that is life will die."

We just learned that our daughter, Erin, is self-quarantining. Although receiving a false-negative, the doctors feel that she has COVID-19 symptoms. She doesn't need to be hospitalized but must remain bedridden for the time being. We call and pray, pray and call. Visits are out of the question. Seven weeks after the viral onset, our beloved Erin is recovering . . . ever-so slowly. Our prayers continue.

There's more. I'm writing in the midst of a universe groaning and aching with illness and death, and we're welcoming, as the Spring Equinox arrived (March 20, 2020), our very first great-grandchild: Kaliyah Monteen Chapman Taylor in Portland, Oregon. Cheers, dear one! Everyone is healthy, thus far. This reminds me of the Japanese concept of *shoji* which illustrates that living-and-dying are joined as holy forces.

Mainly, I'm wrangling with the unavoidable reality of death in my own clumsy, driven way: writing, writing, writing, writing away on this "critical" book.

The observation of author Annie Dillard is hauntingly apt: *Write as if you were dying. At the same time, assume you write for an audience consisting solely of terminal patients. That is, after all, the case. What if you began writing as if you knew you would die soon? And what could you say to a dying person that would not enrage by its triviality?*

Writing is my main mode of con-solid-ating my scattered emotions and notions, of caressing life's craziness, as I meander through this labyrinth toward the finish-line. We will all die, one day or another, but those tragically infected with COVID-19 have been blindsided. And if they die, they won't likely have had reasonable time to prepare. They won't be reading books or sharing conversations on death, and most agonizing of all, won't be enjoying access to either their chosen life-passions or intimates.

Which makes it all the more important that, when we're conscious and vital, we are willing to face, no embrace, the sovereign truth of all existence: death. In so doing, our life will assume a fresh sense of clarity and urgency. When we "consent to die" (poet W. H. Auden's evocative phrase), we're motivated, indeed freed, to complete our lives as purposefully as possible. We're empowered to stay evergreen.

Of course, I might have waited until my upcoming 80th birthday, or even later, to convey my last hurrah or hallelujah, but you just don't know how many annual go-arounds you'll get, do you? Both my dad and father-in-law died at 81½, the average life-expectancy for men. Who can guarantee that I will live longer than they did?

My two best male friends died recently, one eagerly wanting to halt a pain-saturated existence and the other one, passing away prematurely of an unexpected illness. This present volume partially arises out of my own grief. We had covenanted for both of these brothers to speak at my memorial service, but, lamentably, I ended up speaking at theirs. This duo of heart-wrenching deaths has placed my own impermanence front and center. Accordingly, this book furnishes a modest tribute to Nathan's and Paul's ongoing presence in my remaining years on earth. It aspires to validate the sentiment of Thornton Wilder:

There is a land of the living and land of the dead. The bridge is love; the only truth, the only survival.

Only love conquers death. These buddies, and countless others, won't return in person, only in love. Only in love do I have them still.

I'm also writing about this taboo topic, since the very religion which I've served as a ministerial practitioner for 50 years, would do well to address more keenly the manifold personal, relational, and spiritual issues of dying and death. Our appreciation of "earth-centered traditions" would beckon Unitarian Universalism to acknowledge life *and* death as fused realities in "the sacred circle of life." However, nowhere in our primary theological document (Article II—Purposes and Principles) is there any explicit recognition of our human finitude and mortality.

From 2003-2009, I was privileged to serve on the *Commission* on *Appraisal* for the UUA; our mission was to update our governing principles and sources (adopted in 1984). During a comprehensive six-year process, we received hundreds of constructive recommendations focusing upon unaddressed religious themes such as beauty, evil, forgiveness, God, and death . . . especially, death. It appeared that the majority of our membership no longer wished to skirt the topic and were hoping that our progressive tradition would finally celebrate death as a sacrosanct passage.

But that hasn't happened yet . . .

There's mindful meditation, mindful eating, mindful parenting, mindful walking, mindful partnership, mindful work, mindful suffering, and yes, there's mindful dying. It transpires whenever we ponder, plan, and cozy up to our very own mortality—philosophically, pragmatically, and playfully. Mindful dying has proven to be an empowering, comforting, and even enjoyable process as testified to by participants in my workshops. I have seldom experienced such exceptional attendance and expressed gratitude throughout my entire career of conducting adult programs. Mindful dying resounds with the soulful desires and needs of fellow wayfarers.

Plainly, I'm neither a scientific investigator nor a professional *thanatologist*. I'm a pastor, and my advice is straightforward: whatever the manner or date of our extinction might be, it behooves us to reflect deeply and prime diligently for our death, while we're still awake and kicking. May we refrain from taking a spiritual bypass and face our own end as boldly and creatively as possible. Doing so will deliver unspeakable gifts both to ourselves and to our loved ones.

Making Peace with Our Own Death may become one of the most important things we will ever do.

CHAPTER TWO

Embracing Our
Mortality

*In truth, everything arises in order to disappear:
everything we have, everything we think we are,
must at some point be surrendered, for it is only
on loan from the bounty of the Divine.*
—ALISTAIR SHEARER

My religious tradition matured considerably when dealing openly
and caringly, during recent decades, with the AIDS deaths of our
own members as well as community fellow travelers. Unitarian
Universalism, in countless villages, stood out as a site that would
properly serve and memorialize those who fell to this dread disease. One of our gifted and beloved ministers, Mark Mosher de
Wolfe (1953-1988), in a sermon preceding his own death to AIDS,
penned these words:

It takes courage to live in the face of death. The sources of such courage are not in the outside world, they are not in special rev-elations or in the inspirational messages of gurus. The sources of courage are found in the inner soul, nurtured with love, inspired by faith, united in the worshipping heart.

Making Peace with Our Own Death claims unequivocally that death is real and to be treated as such, particularly amidst our death-defying culture. Our bodies, which are made of the earth, will, in due course, return to the earth; we travel from dust to dust. We pronounce in Unitarian Universalist memorial celebrations, at the very outset, that "Josephina Doakes has died; you and I are alive," so we know who's still breathing in the room and who isn't. The spirit may endure, but the body of the dead person exists no longer, and that difference is saluted rather than camouflaged in euphemisms like "she's gone away" or "he's passed on."

I grow exasperated when at the three nursing homes where I sing weekly (pre-COVID-19), "death" is so frequently veiled. When I ask about someone who's missing, I often get the brush off. Only, as I'm about to leave might a professional whisper in my ear that either Jorge or Margaret has "expired." Licenses expire; people die. If there's any place where death should be treated frankly, yet tenderly, it's in a nursing home.

Death cannot be tamed. Death is mysterious. Death is death, and a key to living fully is acceptance of that fact. As our Unitarian Universalist poet laureate, Ric Masten, used to bellow: "Hey, folks, remember that we're all terminal on this ward!" and as another associate mulls: "Death might not be the end of my story, but it's certainly the close of a substantial chapter!"

Just when we're prone to deny or tame death, just when we

think we can outwit or beat it, death comes up and bites us in the butt. Generals and domestics, reverends and school teachers, presidents and plebeians are bitten. It's sobering to realize that no matter our wealth or status, trophies or burdens, our eventual fortunes are equivalent.

The universal law of reality is impermanence: everything is in flux and change. Existence exudes an incessant arising and fading away: birth, growth, decay, and death. When Buddha was dying, he lay down on the ground in front of everyone and spoke candidly: "Don't look away. You too, will be like this one day!" Mortality is the one feature all living entities share in common. Let us heed the counsel of the World Health Organization: "World death rate is holding steady at 100%."

I used to be mystified by the ancient practice of greeting people with the words, "Memento Mori" or "Remember Death." Medieval folks struck me as an oppressively morbid bunch, yet, in my eldering years, I've come to appreciate their standpoint. After all, they experienced plagues and fires, wars and devastation. They knew first-hand—that just as life abounds, so does death—that there is no light without shadow. *Memento mori*, fellow pilgrims, *memento mori!*

Recall the death of Moses. He was 120 years old at the time and had led an extraordinary life: everything from freeing his people from slavery to spending forty full years in the desert. But how does this spiritual giant die: alone on a mountain overlooking the very Promised Land that he would never enter?

Death will snatch us away in its own time and inscrutable fashion—maybe painful, maybe soothing—but death is not mean or an outlier or a failure, neither an enemy to be conquered nor a prison to be escaped. Death just is, as life just is: a series of transitions, one after another—colossal, tiny, awkward, and desirable ones—culminating in the transition of transitions.

As bard Anne Sexton (1928-1974) put it: "Someone has died, even the trees know it." Yes, the dogs smell our death, insects are on alert, the wind grasps every fatality, and "the trees know it." When these kinsfolk are lugged away into lumber, may our human hearts venerate them.

Death's not only inevitable; it's also natural in the overall sweep of things.

About 500 million years ago, all of life was composed of algae and amoebas, of a unified, continuous existence, growing at one end and sloughing at the other. Into that world of endless glop came the transfiguring event of death. Without death, life could never have risen out of the immortal slime. Now, death and life are inextricably linked; both constitute necessary and sanctified gifts of one supreme reality.

Moreover, death is desirable (at least for those who have been graced with a sufficient number of seasons) as well as inevitable and natural. Death's presence intensifies both our capacity to love and our impulse to create meaning and beauty. Life possesses urgency and importance, because we won't always be around. We squeeze life all the more, since it's limited.

A brief snapshot from my own pastoring. When I entered the ministry I was guided, if not driven, by the prompting: "Hey, I've got to love." Now, nearing the culmination of both ministry and existence, I realize that my early inducement was a bit confused and compulsive. I now know that "I get to love." Every additional day of living and loving is an unmerited gift of grace.

Whelmed by the affection of spiritual kin and immersed in the divine love dwelling at the heart of Creation, I am pulled by gratitude, not pushed by approval, and freed, rather than obligated, to love. Maturing from the pressure of "I've got to love" to the blessing of "I get to love" has made an immeasurable difference in the carriage of my sojourn on earth. I feel more liberated and relaxed as I conclude both ministry and life.

As we round life's unfolding bends, we personally begin to realize, given the cosmic sweep of things, that our discrete lifetimes have been relatively brief. We have 10, 20, maybe 30 autumns remaining, so the final assignment means coming to grips with our transience.

We wish to travel on home as unencumbered as possible. One of our close ministerial associates was Clarke Dewey Wells (1930-2006) who eloquently described the art of shedding:

One definition of sin and idolatry is being weighed down with so much luggage we lose the purpose of the trip. David went against Goliath leanly prepared. He did not accept the proffered armor. It would have been his death. And the saints? They travel light. That way they can look and see and relate and heal. That way they can hear the music and dance.

Daily, we elders must ask ourselves: what might be weighing us down? What debris can we discard right now from our personal, relational, and professional cargo?

Shedding objects and dreams is one thing, shedding our preoccupations and obsessions is yet another, but shedding our body, the same shell we've carted around all our waking moments—for better and for worse—poses a heftier challenge. Death comprises the passage where we lose our corporal incarnation, lose our consciousness, lose our connectedness, and, altogether, lose our known universe. Life's ultimate surrender requires letting go, letting be, and letting come…as we voyage toward an infinite surprise.

As expected, this transition is fraught with complications. There exist comrades who engage in what might be called a hasty release. Once they reach roughly their fifties, they seem to live with one foot already planted in the grave. Every trouble or torment spells, for these folks, a death warrant. They mistake resignation for surrender. They're numbered among the walking dead; they've lost perceptible lust for life.

My cousin Rene Zendejas was the exact opposite. He kept fighting every mounting loss, since, in some weird way, Rene believed he was deathless. As he put it: "Tommy, I plan to be immortal now, not later!" Possibly, there have been times when you or I have also felt immortal. However, life, to be finished well, demands a willingness to embrace our mortality. To do so actually heightens our sensitivity to the preciousness of every instant.

Psalm 90 announces that humans are akin to grass, that the years of our lives may be three score and ten, or, with luck, four score and more. Everyone dies, sooner or later; thus, the Psalmist goes on to admonish: "Teach us to number our days that we might apply our hearts unto wisdom." This passage bids us to absorb every hour of existence—its sorrows and joys and blends thereof—with faithfulness and mettle.

Whatever our personal view of post-death might be—resurrection of the body or immortality of the soul, reincarnation or an eternal abyss—there manifestly comes a time of physical cessation, when we no longer amble this earth in our present bodily form.

Mortality cannot be dodged. At some juncture, we must admit that death is natural, often safe, and that we cannot fail at it.

When's the optimal time to die? Of course, it depends upon circumstance and condition. Your timetable may not match mine. However, we all would likely concur with the outlook of Henry Cadbury, distinguished scholar and teacher, who lived well into his nineties. When asked how he felt about the prospect of his death, Cadbury replied with a knowing smile: "Well, I don't want to live too long, and I don't want to die too soon." To die sometime between too long *and* too soon should prove just about right. If we're lucky, that's how we'll greet our demise.

In any case, when we make peace with our own death, we're frequently filled with a feeling of relief; we're able to surrender to the cosmic mystery. Along with Jesus of Nazareth, we can say: "It is finished." The Jewish prophet was urging home-stretchers to tie up loose ends and to resolve unsettled matters—in sum, to apply the finishing touches to our earthly trek. We all hanker for some measure of graceful wrap-up. A measure, I say, because we usually exhale with one thing or another incomplete, don't we?

Surrendering is such an awkward art to master—excruciatingly so for high-control, hyper-questing pilgrims. It requires a delicate mixture of being passive yet staying active. Surrendering isn't resignation but acceptance and requires immense courage. It means letting ourselves be who we presently are, rather than clinging to what we used to be or might have become. Surrendering entails heeding the universal wisdom in this simple maxim from the 700 verse Hindu scripture, *The Bhagavad Gita*:

Do your duty without attachment to outcome.

Surrendering means permitting ourselves to decelerate and to tolerate our own age and condition . . . as dynamically as possible. Surrendering entails our relinquishing "stuff" as well. As I've been drawing my full-time ministries toward completion, I've undertaken a massive trimming program: ridding myself of 90% of my books, 70% of my files, and half of my professional collectibles.

I've done this for several reasons. Foremost, I desire to journey less laden through my homestretch laps. I also enjoy placing professional treasures directly into the hands of up-and-coming colleagues who might relish them. Of course, I'm making mistakes; there are possessions I should have kept and paraphernalia I've already missed. So, it goes; that's the gamble of shedding.

Futile dreams, harmful biases, and festering emotions need to be shorn as well. Surrendering has everything to with interior mop-up, releasing obsolete and damaging memories—a crucial route toward en-*lighten*-ment. The nightfall of existence is arguably the best season to reflect, sort out, and choose only what seems worthy of our humanity.

It's told of the spiritual master Jiddu Krishnamurti that when he was quite old and frail, he happened to be lecturing to a large assembly with customary gentleness. Jiddu recognized a questioner slowly, indeed haltingly; then he tried to respond to the woman in the audience. When Krishnamurti was unsuccessful in launching a dialogue, he abruptly stopped, and conceded that he wasn't mentally sharp anymore; so might the woman please come down to the front and just hold his hand for a while, in reverential silence? What an exquisite example of conscious surrender: emptying one's self of former faculties and opening to the unfathomable now.

As we maintain faith in the flow of life's final curriculum, we're able to welcome whatever sacrifices and secrets unfold . . . accept even death itself. In surrendering back to the Infinite Spirit of Life and Love, submission isn't required, but trust is. We give ourselves *over* rather than away.

From midlife forward, we finally grasp the certitude that every love relationship ends in a loss: through divorce, departure, or death. We will die, and so will our comrades and loved ones. As we open ourselves to the precarious depths of love, we bare ourselves to the raw torment of loss. We even experience those we've cherished oft-living on in our souls after their earthly departures. I value the way our friend, the Rev. Forrest Church, phrased it during his own rapid weakening and premature death: "The love we have given to others is the one thing death can't kill." Or in the words of St. Paul: "Love never ends . . ."

There's more heartening news contained in our Unitarian Universalist gospel. Just as we were graciously ushered into being, as a gift beyond our earning, so also there will be Love awaiting us after we die. There is no need to discuss or debate the particular form such Love might take. No one knows. It's only important that we declare with unshakable fervor and hope that the very Love that created us will surely comfort and cradle us beyond our death . . . into illimitable seasons. The bottom line: we'll be alright when we die.

Buddhists further claim that whereas death marks the end of our bodies, indeed the end of our individual personalities, it most assuredly doesn't signify the end of our existence. When our bodies cease to function, our core merely returns to the source of consciousness or as Unitarian precursor Ralph Waldo Emerson (1803-1882) asserted: our souls are reabsorbed into the eternal Oversoul.

The *chi* (xi or ki) or distinctive life-energy each of us embodied during our earthly existence flows back toward the center of the universe. The whole of cosmic reality is altered, because our unique being was present upon the earth for a spell.

Death is an uncharted universe, a place our intellects can't adequately understand. Unerringly, over half of us are touched every year by the death of a close family member or friend; 10% of us will die suddenly; 90% of us will face pivotal decisions about health care and end-of-life care; and 50% of our medical costs are incurred in the last year of life. And, here and now, we (mainly seniors) hover perilously amidst the COVID-19 calamity, with the global death-count mounting hourly. In the face of such stark realities, *Making Peace with Our Own Death* charges us to wrestle painstakingly, in trustworthy circles of compassion, with honest and heartfelt questions before we die, in order to realize a potentially more serene and satisfying departure.

On the property of First Unitarian Universalist Church of San Diego, where Carolyn and I served for 24 years as co-ministers, we were favored with a spacious courtyard featuring a magnificent terra-cotta Memorial Wall with the names of dead First Churchers (from still-borns to nonagenarians) inscribed upon small-sized tablets. Whenever we met with new members, we would talk first about how our religious tribe might feed their souls, then we would discuss what specific gifts, financial and otherwise, they might wish to bring to our beloved community.

At the close of every session, we would take a walk outdoors and meander through the beautiful grounds to the edge of our canyon and gaze downward upon a labyrinth, manifold botanical species, and perhaps catch sight of an animal or two, as well as soak in a panoramic view of uptown San Diego. And we would sometimes proffer a sermonette: "On this sacred site we have scattered the cremains of dearly beloveds of First Church. Let us thank our spiritual kin for their generous service, as we sit upon their proverbial shoulders and extend our own witness throughout the vineyards of San Diego and beyond!"

We weren't done with our walk. Gently placing foot in front of foot, in meditative fashion, we strolled back up to the Wall: "Before we part today, we wanted to insure that you, our newest members, had a chance to meet previous adherents of our living tradition . . . First Churchers who conscientiously tilled this hallowed ground until the very day they died."

Our Memorial Wall has remained a monument of remembrance for over 40 plus years. Examples abound. One mother, whose youngster was riding a bicycle and hit by a car, would take lunch breaks and visit our wall to pay homage to her dead child. A couple spent the concluding laps of their own lives overseeing the final touches of the Memorial Wall project, then invited parishioners to join them in purchasing plaques. Their loving labor was saluting their son who had committed suicide in his early twenties. Every plaque exudes a distinct and treasured story.

Additionally, the Wall has proven an equalizer in honoring the worth and dignity of members and friends of our congregation: no fancy epitaphs, only the full name, plus the birth and death year, of each deceased are registered upon each, same-sized plaque. After all, are we not equally valuable beings in the eyes of Everlasting Love?

In the end, death's justice comes to everyone in order to make room for other creatures to birth on the scene. We resonate with the way naturalist essayist Wallace Stegner (1909-1993) phrases life's conclusion, during a mellow conversation with his friend James Hepworth:

I've been lucky. I came from nowhere and had no reason to expect as much from this one life as I've got. I owe God a death, and the earth a pound or so of chemicals. Now let's see if I can remember that when my time comes.

We owe—God, this indescribably marvelous universe, ourselves, and all creaturely companions—one death, especially following a blessed and generous ride. May this debt be willingly and gladly paid, when our turn comes to re-enter the ground of all being.

I say gladly, because we're placed on earth to find and deliver joy. And when our light finally goes out, if we're fortunate, our souls will echo the glorious and comforting passage of scripture from Isaiah 55:12—skillfully scripted upon our very Wall:

For you shall go out in joy and be led forth in peace, the mountains and the hills before you shall break forth into singing, and all the trees of the field shall clap their hands.

CHAPTER THREE

An Ever-Evolving Love

Turning to Unitarian Universalism for Grounding and Guidance

We Unitarian Universalists must never forget that
"love is the doctrine" of our church; so we
measure all the seasons of our lives in love.
—THANDEKA

Even for those among us for whom "lines have fallen in pleasant places" (Psalm 16:6), there remain issues to resolve, regrets to release, and promises to satisfy during our denouement. The objective of *Making Peace with Our Own Death* is ensuring that our final laps on earth be meaningful ones: soaked in measures of grace, authenticity, generosity, thanksgiving, kindness, and acceptance.

The challenge is to *fulfill* rather than merely preserve our lives. As we enter our waning years on earth, our foremost assignment sticks: growing, evolving, and abiding in an *ing* condition. Expansive living is a form of transcendence. We are summoned to complete our single existence in an awakening and amplifying state.

When well-utilized, Unitarian Universalism can assist us, both theologically and practically, in the arduous yet holy undertaking of our last hurrah. For inspiration, we will explore two core pillars of wisdom, one rooted in Unitarianism (*"semper reformanda"*) and the other culled from the Universalist legacy ("everlasting love"). Joined together, these principles produce what I'm calling "an ever-evolving love." May we turn to both traditions for spiritual grounding and guidance, as we move inexorably toward our finish line.

"SEMPER REFORMANDA"

Since the universe always changes, the truth about it must change too.
So I need not be ashamed or terrified when my own religious vision changes.
It'll just be me, being part of the universe. Could the universe itself, in all its changing, teach us that security lies not in stasis, but in process?
—Judith Walker-Riggs

The cornerstone of our progressive theology is evolution. It constitutes the way we do religion: be it our organization, our philosophy, our activism, or our eschatology—the science of last things. It's recounted that during the great debate of 16th century

Transylvania, folks scoffed at Francis David for being so change-able. "Look at this David," they taunted; "he starts out Roman Catholic, becomes a Lutheran, then a Calvinist, and now he calls himself a Unitarian. What will he conceivably be tomorrow?" To which David is reported to have said: "*Semper reformanda*" or "always reforming." Perpetually growing in his theology, David became a proponent of religious forbearance for all faiths . . . an utterly radical position in the 16th century Western world.

In those days, religion was a matter of life and death, with formal public debates being held regularly—in this specific case between a defender of the Trinity, Peter Melius, and the advocate of the Unity of God, Francis David. Their fierce dispute ran for ten days, starting at 5 a.m. each day. Placed in perspective, on good days (pre-pandemic), 5 a.m. is the time I might arise to go to the gym for a work-out, rather than bounding up to engage in theological discourse! And our weighty, national political debates, throughout American history, pale in comparison. It took two days merely to establish the ground rules for the Melius-David confrontation.

In fact, before the contest, Melius said to David, "If I win this debate, you will be executed." David calmly retorted, "And if I win this debate, you and everyone else in this land will be given the religious freedom and tolerance due every human being." What an earth-shaking variance in theology, one desperately needed today, when dogmatism and bigotry create massive divisions in our own homeland. Fortunately, David won, and many were converted to Unitarianism, including John Sigismund, the king, who immediately issued the Western world's first edict of religious toleration in 1568. In addition to *semper reformanda*, David also preached "not to think alike but to love alike." Hence, evolving love, not an unbending creed, was the reigning principle of our Unitarian roots. And Hosea Ballou, our Universalist forebear, in 1803 seconded the motion:

> *Let love continue. If we agree in love, there is no disagreement that can do us any injury, but if we do not, no other agreement can do us any good . . . Let us endeavor to keep the unity of spirit in the bonds of peace.*

So, love is the first and last word of both sides of our history, Unitarian and Universalist. Divine and human love, coupled together, provides the ruling energy of our religion.

Sadly, the period of religious openness was short-lived, for John Sigismund, a frail but noble monarch, died three years later in 1571. A repressive emperor followed and summarily dismissed David as the court preacher and imposed censorship against any form of religious free thought. Since David was considered an unrepentant "innovator," he was banished to the dungeon, where he died in 1579 and was buried in an unmarked grave.

Semper reformanda prevails to this day in our ranks. The full phrase, "*ecclesia reformata et semper reformanda,*" means "the church reformed and ever needing to be reformed." This mandate pertains to both individuals and communities. Furthermore, it challenges adherents to be recipients as well as makers of change.

In short, we are summoned to be bi-lateral in our evolutionary growth. Whenever surveys have been taken in our reformist tradition, various words and phrases pop up such as quest, transformation, search, evolution, metamorphosis, growth, "changing ourselves in a changing world" (the motto of Meadville Lombard Theological School), "nothing is settled, everything matters," "revelation is not sealed," and "the way leads on" (Edwin Muir, #670 in our hymnal). Our faith forthrightly contends that all reality is arising and disappearing, unfolding and advancing. And so are we humans—being verbs more than nouns. So the gerund-emphasis of *Making Peace with Our Own Death* stands in strong alignment with our theology.

Every hour holds some deepening claim, corrective slant, and improbable surprise. We are not limited by past mistakes or present prejudices. We are born over and over again, not just once or twice; then we die, somewhere in the middle of our voyage, waiting for the unknown to reveal itself. As we say at First UU Church in San Diego when extinguishing our flaming chalice in memory of a deceased member during a Sunday worship service: "In mystery we are born, in mystery we live, and in mystery we die."

Moreover, we are renewable creations. We belong to a springy venture, not a static enterprise. The "interdependent web of all existence" is permeable and fluid. Our religion is anchored to no single moment, no particular guru, and no one pledge but rather linked to countless events, persons, and scriptures. Furthermore, the profundities of the religious life emerge gradually, often with difficulty. As colleague Alma Crawford astutely remarks: "In our tradition, discomfort—like prayer, fasting, and yoga—is a spiritual discipline!"

Another heads-up: time *per se* is neutral, as Dr. Martin Luther King, Jr. noted in his classic 1963 statement from the Birmingham jail:

> There is a strangely irrational notion that there is something in the very flow of time that will inevitably cure all ills. Actually, time can be used either destructively or constructively. Human

progress never rolls in on the wheels of inevitability. It comes through the tireless efforts and persistent work of people willing to be co-workers with the Creation.

King's words are not only perceptive for our ever-evolving anti-racism work (which we've aptly called *Journey Toward Wholeness*) but also prove discerning for every personal, social, and spiritual struggle in which humans are embroiled. Time is impartial; it's what we do personally and societally with our time that matters. That goes for ministry as well.

It's a realistic perspective to concede that every pastorate, whether lasting one year or thirty plus years, has a specific beginning and end. Colleague Rosemarie Smurzynski furnishes a useful reminder: "You are my people and I am your pastor, for a while!" Every ministry is an interim one and to be treated as such. We ministers are not church owners but rather communal stakeholders along with laity. Ministry ultimately resembles life: we end our tenure with certain things completed and others yet to be realized. *Semper reformanda* means: keeping on, keeping on, and keeping on until we die. Then?

If and when a judgment day arrives, the focus won't be on our brilliant or noble thoughts, or even any of our mystical epiphanies, but upon our intrepid acts of joy-sharing, peace-making, and justice-building. Embodiment will be the litmus test of our earthly sojourn. How often did our words become flesh and our resolutions produce deeds?

We seek after the truth, find some, tell as much as we can, and acknowledge that others may have truths that we haven't fully processed. But incarnating truths in our daily lives is the conclusive proof of our humanity. Truth is a verb, and the Christian Scriptures exhort us, above all else, "to do the truth," not just chat about it, pay homage to it, or fuss with it. We're ultimately summoned to be *truthers*. Or as one of my teenage service-partners chuckled: "I'm just trying to follow my feet."

There are examples galore of *semper reformanda* in our progressive heritage. In the suffragist and abolitionist era, women such as Sojourner Truth, Clara Barton, Harriet Tubman, Elizabeth Cady Stanton, and Frances Ellen Watkins Harper were enterprising truth-doers well into their senior years. In large measure, these ardent feminists (many of whom were practicing Unitarians or Universalists) lived energetic and lengthy lives, because they were occupied with sizable spiritual challenges. They stayed morally employed. They kept aroused by asking: "What will best serve the universe today?" rather than fixating upon their own needs. They dismantled their "vertical coffins" and personified meaningful deeds.

Women weren't "given" the vote; they had to march forth and "grab" it. Our fore-sisters knew that progress was not inevitable. You have to make it happen. America stands in 2020, gloriously celebrating the 100th anniversary of women's suffrage, due to dauntless women ancestors harvesting to the end. But the murky struggle wasn't over in 1920. African-American women like Fannie Lou Hamer, Ella Baker, and Diane Nash continued the fierce battle for voting rights for all, culminating in the passage of the Voting Rights Act of 1965. Yet, in 2020, disenfranchisement is alive and well. Voter suppression remains a perilous moral crisis, especially for Black, Indigenous, and People of Color (BIPOC), in our "land of the free and home of the brave."

On the eve of Rosh Hashanah, the beginning of the Jewish New Year, we lost a fiery, brilliant, relentless, and unfailingly gracious Supreme Court Associate Justice and civil rights activist, Ruth Bader Ginsburg. In tribute to this remarkable woman, may we weep heartily tonight, then suit up tomorrow as servants for greater equity and compassion for all.

Semper reformanda.

Mary Livermore, who was born 200 years ago in 1820 and died in 1905, certainly earned the title granted her by Great Britain as "America's Queen of the Platform," because she spoke in Universalist congregations as a layperson at least half of the Sundays as well as lecturing at home and abroad. As chronicler Clinton Lee Scott reports:

Her booking agents warned Livermore against dealing with controversial matters.

She listened but went her own way, speaking on the most divisive questions of the day—women's equality with men, the liquor problem, suffrage, the double standard in sexual morality and marital relations.

American social reformer and "bi-centennialist" Susan B. Anthony (1820-1906) once said that she wished "to live another century and see the fruition of all the work for women's rights." Although she never got the right to vote herself, I have always been inspired by the manner in which she completed her life-journey. During the last 48 hours of her existence, Anthony faintly voiced the names of suffragists who labored alongside her, knowns and unknowns, in a veritable roll call. Susan B. was acknowledging each and every one of her co-conspirators. There's no finer way to finish life than with heartfelt, spoken appreciation.

And we would be remiss, if we didn't pay homage to Judith Sargent Murray, feminist essayist, poet, and commentator of considerable note who died exactly 200 years ago in 1820, the same year that Livermore and Anthony were born. In her essay entitled "On the Equality of the Sexes," Murray wrote: "Yes . . . our souls are by nature equal to yours; the same breath of God animates, enlivens, and invigorates us . . . " Judith was ambitious on her own, while remaining spirited on behalf of her husband, John. Among her admiring subscribers were John Adams, George and Martha Washington, and Benjamin Franklin.

Here's the valiant witness of another feminist honoree. In 1861, Olympia Brown arrived at St. Lawrence Theological School to study for the ministry, startling the seminary President who thought he had discouraged her from enrolling. After becoming the first woman to be denominationally ordained (as a Universalist) in 1863, Brown became an advocate for the right of women to vote. It was not until 1920, at the age of 85, that Rev. Olympia was able to cast her first ballot.

I fondly remember a veteran member, whose grandparents were founders back in 1868, of our UU congregation in Davenport, Iowa, which I served from 1973-1978. In her mid-eighties, Dr. Braunlich started reading Russian novels and studying chemistry, as she couched it, "to fill in the gaps of my knowledge." She wasn't just growing older but becoming *newer* as well. Braunlich would also write critical comments in the margins of my printed sermons and needle me to review them, while I was visiting in her nursing home. In extending her own horizons, sister Alice kept those around her nascent as well.

A delightful scripture on preserving an evergreen awareness is Psalm 92:14 (New Revised Standard Version): "In old age, they still produce fruit; they are always green and full of sap." Or if you prefer the King James Version: "They shall be fat and flourishing." In any case, our final laps are supposed to be generative ones, typically full of sap.

Semper reformanda.

We turn to a telling example from our Unitarian heritage. William Ellery Channing (1780-1842) practiced rigorous spiritual disciplines throughout his life, yet his personal piety was maintained for one reason alone: to effect social change. He directed the substance of his ministerial career not only to informing hearts and transforming souls but also to reforming the structures of society.

Channing's causes ranged from child labor to alcoholism, slavery to juvenile delinquency. He was also deeply concerned for both prisoners and the poor. Flawed, Channing was . . . even reluctant. Yet William Ellery agreed with Emerson that "ideas are tangible things to be lived." So, he lived freedom, lived justice, and lived mercy, however imperfectly.

What's exemplary about Channing was his willingness to progress as a prophetic presence. So, he kept on evolving morally and spiritually all the way to his crypt. Perhaps his foremost growth as a minister occurred with respect to his anti-slavery work. Channing was profoundly impressed with Lydia Maria Child's viewpoints on slavery espoused in the first antislavery book published in America: *An Appeal in Favor of that Class of Americans Called Africans* (1833). Channing was so captivated by Child's book, that, despite ill health, he walked a couple miles to her place to discuss the issue. After a three-hour conversation, William Ellery credited Child with goading his conscience to speak out on the question, even if not as zealously as Child desired. Lydia regularly chastised her religious sympathizers with stinging words:

I find Unitarianism a mere half-way house, where spiritual travelers find themselves well accommodated for the night, but where they grow weary of spending the day.

Never a full-bore abolitionist, Channing pushed to bring an end to slavery in his "calm, self-controlled, benevolent" way. In the final analysis, Channing's views on slavery proved too drastic for the alienated Unitarian conservatives and too tepid for the radical abolitionists. Channing preached week after week to stodgy, stubborn Bostonians nudging the most recalcitrant toward "cheerful, vigorous, beneficent action of each for all." He was a moderate with courage, what progressive theologian Jack Mendelsohn called "a civilized controversialist." Channing embodied ever-evolving love, however tentative and timid.

Evolution has been echoed as well in our Universalist heritage. Benjamin Rush (1746-1813), signer of the Declaration of Independence, physician, social reformer, and enthusiastic supporter of the Enlightenment, always talked about our country's destiny in progressive terms: "A belief has arisen that the American Revolution is over. This is so far from being the case that we have only finished the first act of the great drama." In 2020, when America confronts multiple "revolutions" of moral gravity, it is sobering to recall the sentiments of Rush, an ardent Universalist, affirming that society *and* religion are inherently developmental processes. Both remain incomplete, in full swing, and ever-evolving.

Bill Jones (1933-2012), a leading Unitarian Universalist

theologian, in reflecting upon building bridges of respectfulness across races and cultures, put it succinctly: "The mission of racial justice is nothing less than the co-equality of individuals." I highlight his term co-equality in our quest to stay *semper reformanda*. Dr. Jones contended that neither assimilation nor integration is adequate to the task of fostering principled bonds; only co-equality is sufficient, since it esteems the full worth and value of all persons involved. Co-equality exists when fairness and equity prevail in the minor details of every major task we pursue. Co-equality is what the Buddhists mean when they practice "right relationship."

When Thucydides (460-400 B.C.) was asked if justice would ever come to Athens, the Greek general and historian replied, "Justice will not come to Athens until those who are not injured are as indignant as those who are injured." That ancient contention still rings true in the craggy, steep battle for justice and dignity in our 21st century. And eldering is no era to wallow in neutrality, spectating from the sidelines, because of our age or condition. Instead, it is the season to continue breaking silence and joining in resistance, to keep listening and raising a righteous ruckus. We need to be life-long allies, accomplices, and advocates for everyone who suffers injustice.

An elder of the Achuar tribe of Ecuador, one of the oldest indigenous peoples of South America, upon being offered help by a good-natured, benevolent Westerner, responded in this way:

If you've come to help me, you're wasting your time.
But if you've come because your liberation is tied up with mine,
then we can work together.

The Hindu salutation, *namaste*, says it all: "I honor that which is divine in you, or that place where you and I are one."

Respect literally means "to look at something or someone again." Respectful persons are those who look again at what is easily ignored or missed. We look again at outworn, debilitating patterns and consider developing new habits, even during our final laps. We look again at our own motives before casting judgment on others. Practitioners of respectfulness look again at our history of human brutality and ecological disaster in order to serve and sustain a cosmos moving beyond it.

Humans filled with genuine respect for self and other can look again and again into one another's eyes and say: "You and I are equally worthwhile creations. I hold you in the highest regard. Your time, your tasks, your needs, your capacities, and your identities are as significant as mine and will be treated as such in our relationship. Together we will build, cross, and repair the bridge called respect."

Rev. Joan Javier-Duval pays deep heed to the universal virtues of co-equality and respectfulness in her 2020 General Assembly homily:

Liberation is costly, and it is compelling.
We are drawn towards it for survival.
We are drawn towards it for flourishing.
We are drawn towards it by the bonds we share with one another.

As Unitarian Universalists, our faith compels us towards seeking collective liberation: a liberation that recognizes we are dependent on one another and upon the Earth and that the freedom of any one of us is tied to the freedom of all of us.

Universalist minister, Lewis B. Fisher had heralded a century earlier, in 1921, a parallel sentiment of being "drawn towards" greater justice and liberation:

Universalists are often asked to tell where they stand. The only true answer to give is that we do not stand at all, we move. We grow and we march, as all living things forever must do.

Consequently, we current stakeholders refer to Unitarian Universalism as a *movement* which was recently exemplified when the lyrics of two of our signature songs were amended to describe more accurately our religious sensibility. Rev. Jason Shelton's "Standing on the Side of Love" was altered to read "Answering the call of love . . . " and Pat Humphries' ballad: "We're going to keep on *walking* forward" now says "We're going to keep on *moving* forward . . . " Both were changed to respect those who aren't able to walk without assistance.

For Unitarian Universalists, PC doesn't refer to "political correctness" but instead to our flawed yet persistent efforts to be "personally compassionate," "pluralistically conscious," and "prophetically courageous."

Even as our physical and mental capacities diminish, our souls can keep on progressing, all the way to our coda. Our Unitarian Universalist "good news" invites us to come as we are . . . moving toward who we might become. We are carriers of an ever-evolving love.

Bernice Johnson Reagon of *Sweet Honey in the Rock* singing group fame, as well as long-time UU fellow-traveler, declares: "I'm stubbornly insisting on forward motion." Yes, we move relentlessly toward the growing of a beloved earthly community, wherever we're planted. We golden-agers endeavor to negotiate steady, small advances, as Unitarian Universalist comrade, Joyce Poley, puts it in her ballad, "One More Step" (#168). The word "perseverance" means, in Latin, "one who sees through to the end." Such is the aim of an ever-evolving love.

One of our church members, at the age of 92, phrased it thusly: "I'm constantly reforming, open to new ideas and choices. No surprise. I'm not the same person I was last month!" Wandering and wondering down life's winding pathway, laden with poignant recollections, cruel infirmities, and seaworthy hopes . . . we all journey toward one looming certainty: death.

There's the Zen story of two lost monks, happening upon a crone, an archetypal woman of sagacity. The two ask the one: "Where is the way, the way, the way?" And the crone confidently replies: "Straight ahead!" Whether rejoicing, scuffling, roaming, mellowing, or dying, we are pressed to move straight ahead. At our recent men's renewal (notice we intentionally call them *renewals* rather than retreats!), we were invited to state our wrap-up mission in a few words upon a rock that we had hand-picked from the surrounding wilderness. I inscribed upon my stone: "tenderly . . . homeward!"

John Haynes Holmes (1879-1964), prominent Unitarian minister, pacifist, and co-founder of both the *National Association for the Advancement of Colored People* (NAACP) and the *American Civil Liberties Union* (ACLU), once commented on three kinds of people among the Israelites during their march through the desert.

One group wanted to go back to Egypt. They preferred slavery to the uncertainty of the wilderness. The second group was satisfied with wherever they might camp at night. They were content to gather the manna as it came. The third group, the smallest, wanted to go forward. Moses was among their number. He heard God say: "Speak to the children of Israel that they go forward" (Exodus 14:15), and Moses internalized that mandate. In our own tongue, these are respectively the spiritual and social reactionaries, conservatives, and progressives. They are the people of yesterday, today, and tomorrow. Frankly, over time, I've found myself situated in all three states. Upon more than one occasion, I've felt them battling for ascendancy in my soul. My life sometimes entails being caught in a storm of live coals, hot ashes, and boiling mud, and I struggle to "go forward." How about you?

I grew up thinking that the term Amen meant "so be it," as if we were merely adding an exclamation point to what had just been spoken or sung in community. I have since learned that Amen correctly translates not as "so be it" but as "so *might* it be." Amen refers not to an actuality so much as to an aspiration. Amen isn't another honeyed, superfluous four-letter word thrown in for magical measure. Amen is motivation to translate our yeses into deeds that might, in due course, revitalize the cosmos.

However, an aspiration is not an accomplishment, and our earthly quest is the pursuit of progress not perfection. According to the Genesis story of Creation, when finished, Yahweh said that "it was good, very good." And that pronouncement also encompassed imperfect humans. Good in the biblical sense means: "entirely adequate to its purpose." Hence, while blemished, we're good enough and adequate for what will be required during our sojourn. As my magician mentor nudges: "Tom, never forget that good is better than perfect!"

In the Christian Scriptures we're encouraged to be "whole as our heavenly parent is whole." For centuries, the Greek word *teleios* (which literally means "whole") has been wrongly translated as "perfect;" so countless folks have been swallowed up in a fruitless chase after perfection, resulting in unnecessary personal despair and social havoc. To be a whole person means to own both our good and evil propensities, to accept all of our parts. Note the wisdom of Mona Polacca (1955-), Hopi/Havasupai/Tewa Grandmother, in describing our human condition: "The whole universe is inside every one of us."

Furthermore, as Unitarian Universalists, we proclaim that perfection is an unrealizable goal even when thought of in terms of eons and eons, or endless reincarnations. However, the good news is that only imperfect heartbeats keep us alive. Cardiologists are discovering that the heart approaches a perfect symmetry and balance only a few hours before we die. So, as we live and love, cry and dance, our hearts always contain a slightly irregular rhythm.

I resonate with the statement of colleague, Sean Dennison, in their Berry Street Essay: "A responsible faith dethrones us from the pursuit of perfection and allows us to risk making mistakes, failing." Failing forward is about the best we earthlings can manage, from birth until death. We would do well to quit hounding abstract, platonic ideals, be they of beauty or truth or justice. May we risk swimming the murky waters of reality: making the most of our fragmentary bonds, flawed congregations, faulty resolutions, dysfunctional backgrounds, mediocre jobs, and inexact sciences.

However, despite our imperfections, we keep on loving. I heartily back the directive of Wes Nisker (1942-), Buddhist author, radio commentator, and comedian:

Have a nice millennium, and if you don't like the news,

go out and make some of your own.

There's one thing we progressives have gamely learned: we can't save the world. Not even the most illustrious sages and saints can. The best earthlings can muster is savoring and serving our one and only universe, all the way to our benediction. Truly, if we stay resolute and resilient, we can make some news and become evolving lovers. Being formed in the image of God implies that an unbounded capacity for growth dwells in our very makeup. We human beings are ever-modifying; so is divinity.

Upon encountering the burning bush in Hebrew Scriptures, Moses asks Yahweh for Yahweh's moniker, but the latter only responds with *ehyeh-asher-ehyeh*, which is often rendered by the inert English as "I am who I am." Actually, the phrase translates: "I will become who I will become." God flatly claims to be an unfinished being.

The process philosophers in our ranks have been echoing, prior to the formation of the Unitarian Universalist Association in 1961, but with mounting crescendo ever since, the following argument: because God interacts with the changing universe, God is changeable (that is to say, God is *affected* by the actions that take place in the universe) over the course of time. However, they would aver that the core elements of God (goodness, wisdom, and love) remain intact. God doesn't start earthquakes or administer blindness. The infinite, loving Spirit weeps along with us amidst such inexplicable disasters. Unitarian process theologian Henry Nelson Wieman (1884-1975) dubbed the eternal essence as follows: "God is the growth of meaning and value in the world."

Here's a personal illustration of my own toil with *semper*

reformanda. Throughout my nearly 50 years of doing men's soulful and prophetic work, I have employed the self-identification of WHAAMM: that is, "white, heterosexual, Anglo-American, able-bodied, middle-class, male." A *whaamm* has historically been the premier perpetrator of immense prejudice and travesty throughout the globe. As a member of *whaamm*, I've been a born-and-bred carrier of unearned privilege and power and must labor daily to jettison my very own condition.

Brittany Packnett Cunningham, our 2018 Ware lecturer at General Assembly, exhorts: "The more you benefit from white supremacy, the more you have to be responsible to dismantle it, every single time. You must try to be actively, intentionally, and consistently anti-racist." Henceforth, I'm pledging, as are other self-identified males, to practice the messy, endless labor of dismantling all oppressive systems that keep *us* on top and whaamming away. As a Unitarian Universalist committed to *semper reformanda*, I'm adding an ER on the end of *whaamm* to indicate my commitment to be ever-reforming.

Every day I endeavor to become a whaamm-er. I vow to incarnate a better and braver version of self and ministry, aspiring to observe this razor-sharp demand of our *Unitarian Universalist Ministers Association* covenant:

> *to use our power constructively and with intention,*
> *mindful of our potential unconsciously*
> *to perpetuate systems of oppression.*

To be sure, as a white male elder, my seasons on earth are waning; nonetheless, they remain filled with faith, hope, and love. Despite our 400 plus years of virulent, intractable racism ("America's original sin"), I perceive shining glimmers of promise. The current protests throughout America, in response to the brutal murder of African-American men and women, are essentially peaceful and purposeful. They are not only transpiring in cities but in rural communities as well. Rallies and marches are teeming with greater numbers of "shocked" whites and younger folks than ever before. Even conservative elders like Senator Mitt Romney are showing up. In our laid-back San Diego, an unlikely combo of lawyers, military vets, skateboarders, med students, and surfers are demonstrating. To top it off, individuals in countries around the world are marching in support of human rights in America.

Today's disenchanted ones aren't only engaging in nonstop protest. This newer activist-generation is committed to forging a multi-racial democracy. They are producing worthwhile, follow-up changes; they are both resisting *and* reforming—(knowing well that the word "protest" comes from *pro-testari*, meaning "to testify on behalf of".)

Realizing that tribal prejudices and fears diminish our very humanity, protesters are enlisting as patriotic sentinels to reshape American society. They know that "we repeat what we don't repair." Hence, they are forcing our homeland to be held morally accountable and to take irreversible steps toward paying reparations for African-Americans. They are pushing hard for a "Truth and Reconciliation Commission" on race and policing in America. They are making a lasting commitment to diversity, equity, and inclusion in their larger world. And the spirit of this grizzled civil rights veteran is surging with positivity as fresh troops are fighting anti-blackness, while chanting "we know we will win!"

And just this week, there is hopeful news of the first in a series of lawsuits siding with Standing Rock tribal sovereignty in opposition to the Dakota Access Pipeline. Then there was the favorable decision on behalf of much of Oklahoma still being independent, self-governing tribal land. Remember that in our Declaration of Independence, indigenous peoples were referred to "as the merciless Indian savages on our frontiers."

Joy Harjo, United States poet laureate and member of the Muscogee Creek Nation, believes that this Supreme Court ruling proves the wisdom of her siblings' teachings:

The elders, the Old Ones, always believed that in the end,
there would be justice for those who cared for and who
had not forgotten the original teachings,
rooted in a relationship with the land.

Plus Supreme Court support of rights for both Dreamers and LGBTQIA+ folks—two surprising wins, albeit incomplete. Progressives are also decrying colonialist attitudes and calling for confederate statues to be removed. Tiny and awkward steps, to be sure, but, steps forward toward greater justice and joy. *Semper reformanda.* My heart can't help but hearken back to the words of Meister Eckhart, (1260-1328), German theologian and mystic, who wrote: "Compassion is where peace and justice kiss." Indeed, it is.

I have more hopeful news to report. Our grand-daughter, Corinne, currently teaching ESL in South Korea, is waking up as well. She is joining those who cry out: "We can't change the past, but together we can change the future!" As a young adult Unitarian Universalist, Corinne Chapman is echoing the conviction of Rev. Theresa I. Soto: "All of us need all of us to make it!" Here's but a portion of the passionate letter she penned after the most recent police murders of black Americans:

Hey Gram and Gramp,

Why haven't I been outraged my entire life? It's taken me 22 years to discover the verb in "activism." It's a word that requires action. It's taken me this long to find that being an ally isn't synonymous with being "not racist." And all I can really say to these realizations is: thank goodness it didn't take me a moment longer. 2020 will be the year that we woke up.

Now that I'm awake, I'm learning so much . . . not only about the grotesque, but also about the beautiful as well. I'm learning about the names and faces of the Black trans women that built a safe space for my community and died in pursuit of the rights that I now have today.

Everything that is happening in the US has given me the courage to speak up in my workplace about the racism that I have seen in my time working here in South Korea. Wish me luck with my proposal!

To end on a positive note: I'll be home sooner than we know. I love you so much!

—Corinne

O dear one, your fearlessness is palpable. We can sense your steadfast devotion to restoring the soul of your native soil. And don't worry about your age—John Lewis was one of the original Freedom Riders at the age of 21, served as the "conscience of Congress" for 34 years, and was writing legislation to secure voter's rights the week before he died at the age of 80. Corinne, simply join Lewis and others in becoming a "lifer" for greater freedom and justice. Just keep crossing bridges until your final breath. Ever-onward, *semper reformanda* in the name of love, Corinne—stay "woke."

But the question persists: how can a white, male, geezer currently contribute? Well, for starters, I can listen empathetically to BIPOC siblings, heeding what they specifically want and need. I can participate in our UUA-sponsored "Beloved Conversations" series which occasions painful yet substantive discussions about race. And when the right moment calls, I can support with time, talent, and treasure anti-racist programs and policies in our larger world. A new and better America is in the throes of being born, and I can assist, however modestly, in its delivery . . . rather than settling for being another, old, white guy laden with guilt and fragility!

I can choose to don a *Black Lives Matter* wristband daily. Why? Because all lives won't matter until black lives matter! Why? Because wearing this slim, cotton bracelet reminds me as a *whaamm-er* to relinquish privilege and redistribute power with persons of color and indigenous peoples. Why? Because placing it on my body prompts me to risk living beyond complicity and complacency. Why? Because I desire to be color-sensitive rather than be color-blind. Why? Because solidarity with the oppressed bears witness to "an ever-evolving love!"

Contemplate the weighty statement of our pre-eminent Unitarian preacher and abolitionist Theodore Parker (1810-1860):

I do not pretend to understand the moral universe: the arc is a long one; my eye reaches but little ways. I cannot calculate the curve and complete the figure by the experience of sight; I can divine it by conscience.

And from what I see I am sure it bends towards justice.

I, too, affirm that the moral arc of our universe bends towards justice, but I'm not brash enough to believe that it will do so without tons of human bending, mending, and extending of that same arc. I presume God is doing God's part; are we doing ours?

As the death toll of the COVID-19 pandemic rises, there is much talk, both within and beyond religious circles, about our dwelling amidst an apocalyptic time—the end of the world we've grown accustomed to know. A close colleague, Dr. Frank Placone-Willey, has brought to our attention the fact that the word *apocalypse* literally means "out of concealment." It comes from the Greek word (*apo-kaluptein*) which refers to reality uncovering, unveiling, or unfolding itself. Apocalypse is synonymous with a revelation not previously known and one that allows for positive meanings and results.

In the biblical Revelation of John, apocalypse indicates a cataclysm in which the forces of good permanently triumph over the forces of evil. It is a revelation of godly purpose in union with human agency. Or as we Unitarian Universalists might offer: the true apocalypse will unveil divine-and-human teamwork in building a more just and joyful world.

I often drive by a street corner where a homeless woman daily holds high a sign stating the biblical phrase: "God is able." I always display the peace sign, as well as occasionally give her some money with an info card about the resources of our nearby Rescue Mission which provides nightly shelter and food. She warmly reciprocates. But if I had my druthers, I would amend her sign to read: "God is able, and so are you and I! Together, we make quite a team!" Too often, we humans give total credit to God while dismissing our own power, beauty, and competence.

This mission of divine-human collaboration is reminiscent of the Universalist communal pledge composed by L. Griswold Williams (1893-1942) in 1933 and used regularly in our present-day congregations:

Love is the doctrine of this church,
The quest of truth is its sacrament,
And service is its prayer.

To dwell together in peace,
To seek knowledge in freedom,
To serve human need,
To the end that all souls shall
grow into harmony with the Divine—

Thus, do we covenant with each
other and with God.

To be sure, this current pandemic is a disaster of catastrophic proportions causing enormous fear, loss, and destruction across the globe. But the spiritual challenges posed by an apocalypse are utterly germane as we boldly dare to reset, even restore, the cosmic order.

It is unlikely we will return to physical, economic, social, or medical normalcy—soon or ever—but a series of crucial questions arise: might this be the golden opportunity for humanity to create a new moral state of increasing mercy and justice for all? Or will we blithely resume continuation of world-wide greed and xenophobia? Will this apocalyptic moment motivate us to foster greater international peacefulness and, finally, address climate change and global warming? Will this turning point in human history arouse us to undo our inherited structures and conditions of oppression or will we carelessly succumb to the old *normal* where the least, lost, and last among us are heartlessly exploited?

Of course, especially for the seniors among us, time is running on and out, but will we vow to personify a religion serving the common good until our finis? Will we join forces with the Eternal One?

The astute and kindhearted words of President Abraham Lincoln's First Inaugural Address in 1861, delivered on the eve of the Civil War, come to mind:

We are not enemies but friends. Though passion may have strained, it must not break our bonds of affection. The mystic chords of memory will swell when again touched, as surely they will be, by the better angels of our nature.

No matter how divided and demoralized our country is during this season of a harrowing pandemic and savage racial oppression (bedeviled by both virus and violence), hurricanes and fires, we are summoned to embody "the better angels of our nature." If not now, when?

Former President Jimmy Carter, a dedicated Christian, humbly states: "My faith demands that I do whatever I can, wherever I can, whenever I can, for as long as I can, and with whatever I have to try to make a difference." Truly, any religion that expends every ounce of energy to make the universe a wee bit better . . . constitutes the real thing.

There's a relevant phrase in Hebrew Scriptures, *hineni* which denotes, "Here I am . . . " a word Abraham says to Yahweh three times while navigating serious ordeals. It means he's present and accounted for, ready to do what needs to be done. Abraham refuses to hide; his life will be lived openly. *Hineni* . . .

Few of us, particularly as our energies wane, can change the world as substantially as we used to do. And we aren't replicas of others. However, most of us, until our dying day, can alter the global situation more than we ever dream, if we are but daring and caring and sharing. Instead of waiting to do the one great deed, let's be willing to perform several decent, good acts prior to our extinction. Let's stand equipped and willing to clean up a couple of the messes in our own locality, in the year 2020. We will be heartened by the results, and the whole earth will rejoice along with us.

Former Vice-President Hubert Humphrey (1911-1978) nearing death, addressed the United States Congress with these profound sentiments:

> *The true moral test of a country is what we do with those at the dawn of life (our children), those enduring the shadows of life (our oppressed), and those entering the twilight of life (our seniors).*

Humphrey's words are posted on my desk lampshade, where I daily greet their aptness and thrust for the living of my own days and nights.

Our progressive faith won't let us give up, give way, or give out. I'll never forget the inspirational message Sonia Sanchez, a leading figure in the Black Arts movement, delivered during our General Assembly Ministry Days: "I'm going to stay on the battlefield until I die." And Sonia Sanchez did. Unitarian Universalism goads us to keep trudging through fair or foul weather, good or ill health. The only way to counter a persistent wrong is with a persistent right.

Yet our religion is pragmatic. While we're not likely to eliminate poverty, racism, or sexism, we're called to chase them all the way to the grave, ours if not theirs. The Talmud rightly frames our home-stretch mattering:

Do not be daunted by the enormity of the world's grief.
Do justly, now. Love mercy, now. Walk humbly, now.
You are not obligated to complete the work,
but neither are you free to abandon it.

We are but short-timers on this terrestrial plane. Each of us is bestowed with partial stewardship of a tiny corner of the planet. Our mission is to become responsible shareholders from birth until death. And when we earthlings fall backward or slump sideways, Unitarian Universalism doggedly replants us on an ever-loving path. In the last analysis, we're not sure of our ultimate destination, so we keep plodding with our eyes glued on the prize, harboring enough suppleness to stay our chosen course. May we make new discoveries, brave an unparalleled direction, and zigzag onward. Grow, grow, and grow . . . all the way to our grave. Wakeful elders harmonize with the African saying that "when someone is dead, their feet are in agreement, for they have ceased moving." Being alive means staying in motion, ample emotion, unexpected promotion, even commotion.

We are ever-evolving lovers on an inscrutable, expanding excursion that will never be completed, only surrendered.

"Everlasting Love of God"

This is the real nature of Universalism; it is a religion of ultimate and overwhelming confidence. It expresses the cosmic security of which we must be assured for joyous and creative living. God is loving; and love is sovereign.
—Albert Ziegler (1911-1991)

I'm an unapologetic Universalist. I concur with the central message of universal salvation that John Murray heralded in his first sermon on American soil at Good Luck Point in New Jersey in 1770. To quote the historical perspective of my ministerial colleague, Dr. Jay Atkinson:

Thanks to John Murray's evangelism and organizational work over the next 20 years, there were well over a dozen ministers by 1790 carrying a new message of hope, courage, and divine love to eager congregations stretching from New England to Philadelphia.

The 20th century Universalist minister and historian, Alfred Cole, imagined the "marching orders" of these universalist evangelists in the following words:

Go out into the highways and by-ways of America, your new country.

Give the people...something of your new vision.

You may possess only a small light but uncover it, let it shine; use it in order to bring more light and understanding

to the hearts and minds of men and women.
Give them, not hell but hope and courage.

Do not push them deeper into their theological despair, but
preach the kindness and everlasting love of God.

Our spiritual ancestor, John Murray was challenged to uncover his own light and let it shine. Likewise, unimaginable sources of light are present in every one of us, during every epoch, just waiting to be turned on . . . or kept on. We don't have to carry the torch of another or bask in the refracted glow of a saint. We've emerged from the darkness of the womb and will eventually reenter more darkness of the tomb. But today, our light remains on. We are luminous. Our lives are "guided by such light as we have." (St. Paul)

I love to belt out the African-American spiritual, alone or in group settings, "This Little Light of Mine," usually adding verses pertinent to the specific location—"over our nursing home, over our family, over San Diego, over the world . . . I'm going to let it shine." My little, hoary light is still burning brightly, and I bet yours is as well. Our light shines whenever we welcome a new neighbor on our block or boldly "green" our side yard. Our light shines whenever we make certain our discretionary money goes to causes and people who need it. Our light shines whenever we smile at our partner or shoulder the burden of someone in need. One of the premier questions to ask ourselves upon waking every morn, particularly during this COVID-19 pandemic, is: "What will light me up today?" And when we're alit, we invariably ignite the radiance of those around us.

And these early Universalist ministers don't close simply with

"Give them, not hell, but hope and courage . . . " according to Cole's preaching commission, but go on with the hopeful words: "Do not push them deeper into their theological despair, but preach the kindness and everlasting love of God."

Divine retribution and human revenge were considered by Universalists to be depraved doctrines. Criminal justice reform was consistently the most unpopular cause undertaken by Universalists and required considerable courage. Their founder, John Murray, had himself been tossed into debtor's prison in London and regularly preached to prisoners in the New World. Our present-day religious commitment to restorative justice dwells in direct sync with our predecessors.

Refusing to believe in eternal punishment, Universalists were branded heretical, irresponsible, and subversive. At certain times they were even shunned from societal tasks, denied positions on juries and the like, because they were deemed immoral. Yet their compassionate anthropology flowed directly from their merciful theology.

What does "the kindness and everlasting love of God" truly signify? It means that regardless of how hard we humans work, we cannot create or earn our salvation, which remains the gracious gift of God. It means that whether hiding or running away, we cannot avoid God's inescapable presence. Even human free will, however obstinate, is no contest for the Universalist deity. It means that no matter how fractious the divisions and how extensive the destruction inflicted in human history, God's love will triumph. "Love is sovereign:" dominant, matchless, and supreme.

Contemporary colleague, Rob Hardies, phrases our Universalist message tellingly:

Love that won't let you down,
Love that won't let you go,
And Love that won't let you off.

We can never repay the Creator, only respond. When we feel unconditionally loved by the undergirding Cosmos, we are filled with hope and activated by courage. We pass God's love on, instinctively yet imperfectly, to soil and sky, animals and plants, and to all living beings who hunger for healing and reassurance. Never before in human history has the need for such a thoroughgoing Universalism been more critical. Our gospel yearns to be universalized.

Back in 1970, I was seeking to minister in a more open-minded and spacious household when I entered our faith through the Universalist door, conferring with the Rev. Harmon Gehr of Throop Memorial Church in Pasadena, California (the city of my birth). My dying hope is to exit through the same entrance. My soul reverberates with the resounding power of the Universalist gospel of "everlasting love."

As a Universalist Unitarian, I affirm the following declarations:

— God exemplifies illimitable love, and we humans fulfill our earthly destiny through acts of an all-inclusive love

— We were born in love—challenged, critiqued, and comforted in love—and will return to the embrace of eternal love upon our death

— Despite our vast human differences, we constitute one civilization

— Virtue is its own reward

— Truth is universal . . . spanning all lands, cultures, and eras

— All souls (encompassing animals and plants) are redeemable and ultimately saved

Universalist General Superintendent Robert Cummins offers a comparable summary in a 1943 address:

Any Universalism worthy of its name cannot recognize divisions between people on the basis of race or class or religion or nationality . . . all are welcome, unitarian or trinitarian, white or colored, theist or humanist, so that whatever exclusion there may be is self-exclusion. A circumscribed Universalism is unthinkable.

I was serving in my first settled post as Minister of Education at Neighborhood Church in Pasadena, California when one Sunday morning, our children were asked to describe the "divine." One youngster in our program remarked that "God was fat." The adults in the room were taken aback by this bluntness, but, upon reflection, we realized the child's wisdom. For certainly, any beneficial version of deity must be big enough to enfold all souls. "Yes, fat!"

Put more classically: the fundamental nature of Ultimate Mystery reveals a fount of universal and boundless love, inclusive of all creatures and endlessly sympathetic. As finite lovers, we become collaborators with the divine in serving and sustaining the cosmos. Such is our Unitarian Universalist gospel.

I grew up warbling the 1950's ballad "Vaya Con Dios," along with Les Paul and Mary Ford. I took it to mean "God be with you," which is every teenager's dream and grown-up's desire. It actually translates "go with God." In other words, it's not a plea for God to take special notice of us, but the imperative for humans to grow in alignment with the divine. As an elder nearing my wind-up, I now sing "Vaya Con Dios" as a ballad to bolster a healthier partnership with the Source of Love.

During the Civil War, church leaders thronged to President Lincoln saying, after deep prayer, they were quite sure that God was on their side. And Lincoln gave them the kind of answer they deserved: "I'm not so much concerned as to ask whether or not God is on my side. What I am concerned with is to try to be sure that I'm on God's side."

Lincoln went on to express the heart of his (and our) liberal and liberating religion in the Second Inaugural Address: "With malice toward none, with charity for all, with firmness in the right as God gives us to see the right, let us strive to finish the work we are in, to bind up the nation's wounds." How morally restorative would such Presidential words be for our torn-asunder country today!

In the famous 13th chapter of I Corinthians, Paul places love at the heart of life's meaning. He acknowledges that pious acts, sacrifices, knowledge, prophecy, ecstatic utterance, while important, are but surface manifestations of the overruling truth of religion: "everlasting love." Paul continues, commencing I Cor. 14 with this summons: "Make love your aim."

One of our ministerial friends, Greg Ward, is a man whom I've been blessed to know ever since he was eight years old, when I served as his Minister of Education some 50 years ago. Rev. Greg has created a litmus test he calls the "Easter Exam," which we're all invited to take and, hopefully, pass every year. This demanding test measures the thickness, depth, and scope of our love. The "Easter Exam" recognizes that love is possible, however grueling, even in a hard and hurting world . . . and especially on a weekend when betrayal, anguish, and crucifixion must be faced and transformed.

And we're called to undergo this love-assessment, the Easter Exam, not just annually but over and over and over again.

Whatever one believes or doesn't believe about the bodily resurrection, our lives are deepened only when we can honestly avow, then embody, that love is stronger even than death, that love outlives death, and that there's not only the life of a Jewish rabbi to confirm this truth . . . but, more importantly, there are moments of proof during our own odysseys.

Here we are in 2020, and even as our physical and mental capacities may diminish (few of us elders possess 20/20 vision any longer!), our souls thirst to dwell in righteous orientation with the principles of Universalism—hope, courage, and everlasting love—which propel us to live beyond privatism, partialism, and provincialism.

Nonetheless, the embers of exclusion smolder in contemporary society. A Princeton Research Center survey recently asked, "Do you think there is a Hell, to which people are eternally damned?" and 53% of the respondents said "yes." Unquestionably, the imagery of hell-fire and damnation still haunts people. Children lie awake at night, sometimes in fear of the final judgment. Adults suffer torments of anxiety on their death beds. The doctrine of hell, however modernized, stands as official Christian dogma.

Universalists, while an undeniably upbeat lot, were hardly blind idealists. The so-called *no-hellites* were no strangers to earthly hells of every variety, some of human creation and others beyond their control. Universalists knew sin intimately, as do we all, but felt that honest self-appraisal and repentance would produce necessary correction. There was no need for additional, let alone prolonged, punishment beyond the grave.

There persists a pressing need, both on the streets and within the spirit, for a merciful and compassionate religion that aspires to reduce, if not quench, the fires of hell during this existence and beyond. Rev. Charles Gaines, who was a comrade of ours, captures the direct linkage between divine and human love with these remarks:

A loving God does not condemn anyone to eternal damnation, and when I apply this concept here on earth, I feel it is my responsibility to work for inclusion on all contexts. Ostracism of any kind is a hell on earth.

Unitarian Universalism remains a realistic religion. It doesn't naively argue that life's hells will be eradicated overnight, in a few weeks, during any regime, or even in the course of our lifetimes. We concede that intractable evil lodges within our carefully crafted institutions as well as within our own virtuous souls. Yet, we charge human beings to evolve lovingly, via successive approximations of goodness, maintaining that compassionate talk and walk can grow some corn, as Native Americans are wont to say.

Our gospel promotes chastened confidence in an age filled with dealers of gloom, purveyors of intolerance, and pushers of sweetness. Jesus often said, "Be of good cheer," but when he did, the Nazarene never used the Aramaic equivalent of "cheerio, cheerio." Like Jesus, we dodge the extremes of cynicism and optimism, while fostering a steadfast hope.

I've always been impressed by the fact that the words *hop* and *hope* come from the same root, one that means to "leap up in expectation." Isn't that precisely how it feels to be stretched physically and lifted spiritually? When I'm hopping about, I'm incorrigibly hopeful, and, conversely, when I'm a hopeful being, my spirit can't cease hopping.

There is more linkage. The Hebrew term for hope has the bedrock meaning of "to twist" or "to twine" and is etymological kin to the word *kivin* for spider web—that fragile, silent network of tiny, interweaving threads. We humans add to "the interdependent web of all existence" even as we are created by it. Being connected to all of life, hopers—as Unitarian Universalist Dr. Bernard Loomer emphasized in his relational theology—are charged "to heal and strengthen that part of the cosmic web where we nest."

"Attention, attention, attention," wrote Zen Master Ikkyu centuries ago when asked to write down the highest wisdom. "But what does attention mean?" pressed his questioner. Master Ikkyu replied, "Well, attention means attention." The etymology of attention comes from the Latin *attendere*, meaning to "stretch." One way or another, in authentic living, our souls are painstakingly stretched. Our hearts and minds, bodies and consciences are stretched as well. Stretching ever homeward.

Hopers are stretchers. Finishing life well means daily stretching *upward* to the sky, *downward* to the earth, *backward* in remembrance, *outward* in compassion, and *onward* toward unfathomable tomorrows. Stretching, stretching, stretching . . . then stretching some more. Which is what I'm doing right now, taking a breather from my writing.

The saints of yesteryear used to aver *solvitur ambulando* or "it is solved by walking." But the time may well arrive when we are physical hobbled, wheel-chair bound, or bed-ridden, and we can't walk. Nonetheless, our spirits can keep circumambulating: hopping and hoping homeward in reasonable fashion. As Universalist minister, Albert Perry, used to bellow: "A hoping heart is the stuff of eternity!" Hopers are *semper reformanda* . . .

And aggressing too, which literally means moving toward a goal rather than away or against it. I'm at peace in my life with the fact that authentic aggression marks positive, moral direct- ness. Aggression refers to focused energy and dynamic boldness. Aggression is not violence wherein we violate persons, objects, or principles, resulting in damage and destruction. As colleague Ron Mazur succinctly put it: "the ultimate human power is to say No to violence!"

Healthy aggression is pinpointing what the Hindu *Upanishads* calls "our deep, driving desires" and then summoning the pluck to epitomize those commitments. It's what Mohandas Gandhi (1892-1956), anti-colonial nationalist and political ethicist, called *satyagraha*, which roughly translates as "soul or truth force." Gand- hi believed that those who choose nonviolence opt for the force of justice, the force of love, the force of noncooperation, the force of redistributing power and privilege, the force of resistance to evil, and the force of imaginative, revolutionary ideas.

Our Unitarian Universalist Men's Fellowship was founded in San Diego upon analogous ideals of forcefulness in 1983. Our organization aspired to be male-supportive, pro-feminist, gay-af- firmative, racially-inclusive, inter-generationally-sensitive, and earth-centered. We were aggressively focused on changing the male reality internally, in terms of society's suppressive stereotypes, and externally, in terms of our oppressive behavior. The intentional mission, of our UUMF, over these decades, has been to foster more emotionally expressive, ethically worthy, and spiritually vital males.

Here's one illustration of our healthy aggression. Countless men in our Fellowship have chosen to place in our wallets a pledge (initially crafted by UUMF member, Tomas Firle), that charges us to employ our hands for embraces, wringing, gardening, caressing, art projects, baking, defiance, and play, but never for damage.

The card reads:

My Interpersonal No-violence Pledge

I SHALL NOT:
— raise my voice or use threats to dominate others
— raise my hands in an intimidating manner
— hit or hurt anyone—physically or emotionally—to get my way

I SHALL:
— seek help when I feel moved to the point of violence
— speak out when I witness abuse by others
— encourage others to take an active stand against violence
— use my hands for healing not harm

Then we sign our names at the bottom of the card. I find it morally invigorating to have such a card butting up against family photos, credit cards, and other wallet miscellany as a constant reminder of what's truly important in my quest to be a more mature male being.

Aggression was also the way of Martin Luther King, Jr. and Mother Teresa, and signals the quintessence of our grown-up selves. Without healthy and holy aggression, our courage chickens out, our love turns sappy, our generosity loses punch, and our justice is skeletal. Progression hankers for aggression, the spiritual neighbor of stretching.

I presently jump-start every sermon and seminar with a patch from Kate Wolf's song *Give Yourself to Love*. Tragically, Wolf died of leukemia at the untimely age of 44, so this ballad stands as a tribute to her courageous and aggressive love.

Give yourself to love, if love is what you're after,
open up your heart to the tears and laughter,
oh, give yourself to love.

And then I seek to *give* myself to such love during the course of each ministerial engagement.

Additionally, I close my pastoral workshops with participants singing our contemporary chant composed by Rebecca Parker (words) and Beth Norton (music):

There is a love holding me/us.
   There is a love holding all that I/we love.
There is a love holding all.
   I/we rest in this love.

As Unitarian Universalists we're concerned about tomorrow and work (as well as play) our tails off to make society more beautiful, just, and joyful, but we relinquish the final results. We contend that all of us are held in the arms of Love, no matter what we've done or not done. *Held* is the operative term. This day, one's entire life, and the full-blown universe are held in the grasp of an infinitely loving power.

"Rest assured" is the Universalist phrase. So we trust, so we affirm.

We spend our entire lives not repaying, which we can't possibly do, but answering life's call with love. Loved, we love in return. Then we surrender our fate to John Murray's ascendant blessing:

Rather there is One who loveth you, with an everlasting love, and who will never leave you nor forsake you.

In their own fashion, Unitarians cherish a matching theological awareness. Unitarianism claims that every *unit* of existence is sacred and to be treated as such. Moreover, the nature of ultimate reality is *unified*, and we are mortal guardians of a *uni*-verse.

Note the words of James Freeman Clarke, 19th century Unitarian pastor:

We speak of going to heaven, as if we could be made happy solely by being put in a happy place. But the true heaven, the only heaven that Jesus knew is a state of the soul. It is inward goodness. It is the Love of God in the heart, going out into our life and character.

Therefore, Unitarian Universalism proclaims an unwavering belief in the unity of reality and the conviction that love is the undeniable character of that reality. And, most notably, I, as one human being, am animated, during my earthly stay, to treat our universe as unified and to add my own ounces of love to the mix. As colleague, the Rev. Mary Harrington, dying of Lou Gehrig's disease, so touchingly put it: "What's the most loving thing I can do, right now?" Such is our central affirmation, blending *semper reformanda* and "everlasting love," calling us to exemplify undying love during our earthly stays. Love begets love. An ever-evolving love is both the path and the destination.

Let me personalize our theology for a moment. Blessedly, Love has been the governing energy of my universe, ever since my birth on October 13, 1941. I say blessedly, because I didn't deserve or earn this condition. It was the gift of grace. As Unitarian Universalist partisan, Kurt Vonnegut (1922-2007), affirmed: "Lucky me, lucky mud!" I entered this world ardently wanted by parents who were in their 30's. Hence, I've always believed, even in the gloomiest of hours, that I possessed bedrock "okayness" and that it was good I was alive. While negotiating life's shocks as well as countless travesties of my own doing, I've been upheld by a replenishable pool of love. I've felt cradled in the bosom of love, both human and divine, from the get-go.

Most of us rarely succumb of a broken heart, but myriad humans enter tombs, full of rubble, pining for a motherly caress before and after valediction. As one who suffered what's been termed "the crime of a happy childhood," I received that motherly caress, not perfectly, but amply nourishing for my journey. I resonate with the mindset of Helen Dunmore's benedictory poem:

Death, hold out your arms for me.
Embrace me,
give me your motherly caress.

I enjoyed more good fortune. I pay immense, loving tribute to my only sibling, Phil, three years older than I, a psychotherapist still plying his trade: counseling corporation heads, star entertainers, and death-row inmates at the San Quentin prison in Northern California. Phil has always modeled for me what it means to be a "care-fronter"—a counseling companion who reinforces the energy and health of his clients rather than compounding their dependencies. He assists them in identifying, then embodying, healing resources within their own psyches. Phil will lift people, but he refuses to carry them.

Every year, my beloved brother and I meet-up in our home-town in Southern California, visit sacred as well as cornball neigh-borhood sites, relive family memories (both good and bad), sleep together in one large bed, counsel one another, sing some of Phil's own ballads, and share notes about how we wish to be remem-bered. He has known me longer than any living being. Although our personalities and worldviews differ slightly, our love-bond is unbreakable. We will never forsake one another. Phil may die first, who knows; but neither of us will ever vacate the heart of the other.

And to my beloved soul-mate of 47 years, Carolyn, here's my poetic tribute based upon the following passage by distinguished American poet and teacher, Gwendolyn Brooks (1917-2000): "You are my harvest. You are my business. You are my magnitude and bond."

although we birthed none of our own
we've reared and continue to be reared by four offspring
our co-ministry has also produced a hefty <u>harvest</u>
since we yoked bodies and souls
we've been one another's main <u>business</u>
covenant of thickest consequence

<u>magnitude</u> matches as well
for no one has proven more sizable and
momentous in molding my curriculum than thou

our <u>bond</u> grows inwardly outwardly upwardly downwardly
all the way home

The defining leitmotif of our marriage and co-ministry has been egalitarianism or relational justice. Proverbs 27:17 declares: "As iron sharpens iron, so one person sharpens another." That's the two of us at our best—"corresponding strengths." To be sure, we've fallen short in heeding our governing mission, but we have usually toppled forward. When we married, we already had four children between us and knew that, whereas we desired to be active co-parents, we would not produce offspring ourselves. Our collaborative ministry would be our procreation.

And so we marched off to a courthouse in Davenport, Iowa to combine our personal and familial histories with our moniker becoming: *Owen-Towle*. Carolyn phrases it movingly: "If we could, we would *capitalize* the hyphen in our last name." Hence, we have aimed—for better, for worse, and forever—to capitalize the hyphen in all that we've been, said, and done.

I also extend an overflowing cup of love to our adult children: Chris, Jenny, Russ, and Erin, who, through our awkward, painful, and triumphant blending as a family, have bountifully affirmed our conscientious co-parenting, from 1973 until this very day. Despite my foibled fathering, our parent-child bond aspires to be faithful, shatterproof, and up-to-date. Unquestionably, parenting has been the toughest and most humbling vocation I've ever undertaken.

Carolyn and I are related to all of our kids—be they natural, adopted, or stepchildren—however, we aren't ultimately responsible for any of them. Incontestably, we have played a critical role in our children's formation, but they possess their own unique personalities and destinies. The desire to re-create one's self through our progeny represents an arrogant and demoralizing blind spot as well as a policy doomed to failure. That's why during child celebrations we often read Kahlil Gibran's declaration of independence:

Your children are not your children. They come through you
but not from you, and though they are with you
yet they belong not to you.
You may give them your love but not your thoughts,
for they have their own thoughts.

The healthiest attitude we parents can muster toward our offspring is what Buddhists call "creative detachment." We aren't the ultimate determiners of our children's identities; they are. We have children on loan, for a while, perhaps 20% or so of their entire lives, bunking at our abode and benefiting from our resources, our counsel, and our gaffes. Then, willingly or reluctantly, we release them to the wider world for their own blossoming. What it comes down to is parents being "adult" enough to proclaim the following: "We have created or launched a life; now let the child (he/she/they) have it."

Our children have inalienable rights to become what they're capable and desirous of becoming, no matter how dissimilar from us or our "virtuous" blueprints. Mature parenting doesn't judge, pressure, over-expect, or control children. Love ultimately accepts their choices and evolution.

Our oldest child, Chris, now 59 years old, shared something beautiful and prescient about "love" way back on his 13th birthday. He penned: "Love is a powerful meaning, and when the powerful meaning is used toward another person, it will raise that person eternally." Note the verb "used." You see, love to be itself must be a verb. It only exists in action. Our youngest child, Erin, was so taken by her older brother's wisdom that, for a while, she had it taped to her bathroom mirror.

I'm taking a time-out, right now, and belting a favorite song of mine: "Everything Possible" composed back in 1983 by UU songwriter and minister, Fred Small, the chorus of which reads:

You can be anybody you want to be;
you can love whomever you will.
You can travel any country where your heart leads,
and know I will love you still.

You can live by yourself,
you can gather friends around,
you can choose one special one.
And the only measure of your words and your deeds,
will be the love you leave behind when you're done.

Small's song provides the motivating ambition of our entire clan: "the only measure . . . will be the love you leave behind when you're done."

But I don't want to over-romanticize either my particular voyage or our Unitarian Universalist course, as we unpack the homestretch aspirations of being an "evolving lover."

Indubitably, as Rainer Maria Rilke noted, "love means holding to the difficult"—not the impossible but rather the unfailingly strenuous. Love is a hard blessing that exacts tough choices rather than indulgent gestures, arousing us to celebrate life intensely even while consenting to die gracefully.

Rilke's all too brief life (1875-1926) comprised an ode to love and its attendant obstacles. Although he matured to stand among the greatest of European lyric poets writing in the years that bordered 1900, Rilke struggled terribly, confessing to being "inept at life." While Rilke's own love life was deficient, he never lost assurance in our human capacity to enlarge the world through loving. Rilke understood that love manifests the central good of human existence, precisely because it is challenging to comprehend and confounding to demonstrate. It's relatively easy to love when we're feeling grand and to disappear when the road gets bumpy. What's demanding is "holding to the difficult"—acknowledging a grisly past, a dreary present, or a forbidding future. "Holding to the difficult" mandates facing another human being with an active gaze and level glance rather than fighting or fleeing.

Love will surely have its smooth—occasional velvety—flashes, but evolving love, over the long haul, requires daily purposefulness. Love is an art, and like other arts, it entails mastery, patience, and exertion. Love has little to do with staying secure and doing convenient things. As author-activist Don Miller says: "When love's a theory, it's safe and free of risk. Love in the brain changes nothing. Love does." If love isn't shared, it ceases to be the real article. Love expends. Love costs. Love loves.

"Love being difficult" impels us to be stout enough to discipline a child, brave enough to navigate painful farewells, and large enough to envelop society's outcasts. Just when we think our task is done, love insists upon yet one more requirement. Just when we are lured to coast in our friendships, love reminds us that more truthful and trusting communication is wanted. Just when we are tempted to draw lines in the sand, love calls us to widen the circle.

Just when we would rather remain comfortably *speciest,* love calls us to recognize the souls of animals. Amidst troublesome life-tussles, love shouts out: "Come on sister, come on brother, and come on neighbor . . . you can do whatever needs to be done. You can do *hard!*"

We earthlings will never experience love in its completeness; at best, we momentarily draw near to its nucleus. It matters not, for our Unitarian Universalist religion commands us to be lifers, ever-evolving lovers, from cradle to crypt. We're in full accord with the 13th century Persian poet Rumi: "Wherever you are, whatever your condition, always try to be a lover."

Semper reformanda.

Writer Eda LeShan (1922-2002) tells the story about a dinner party, when she sat next to a woman who was an oceanographer. At one point LeShan was asked if she had ever wondered why lobsters could weigh one pound, three pounds, even ten pounds when they had such a hard shell. How could they grow? Eda had to tell her dinner companion that resolving this quandary wasn't high on her list of priorities.

The woman smiled and proceeded to explain that when a lobster is crowded in its shell and can't grow anymore, it instinctively travels to some place in the sea, hoping for relative safety and begins to shed its shell. It's a treacherous process—the lobster has to risk its life, because once it becomes naked and vulnerable, it could be dashed against a reef or eaten by another lobster or fish. But that's the only way it can grow.

Plenty of times, Carolyn and I, singly, both as partners and professionals, have known that it was time "to go the reef"—to grow and change, to become more resourceful, more of our better selves.

All of us, periodically, experience a nagging discontent with where and who we are that drives us to the reef, since remaining in a tight shell spells certain stagnation.

Such is the challenge of being homeward bound, making peace with our own death, ever-evolving as a lover. As a staunch Universalist, I believe along with UU songwriter Jason Shelton that "love has already won . . . be not afraid, love has already won . . . " That is our ultimate persuasion; yet, as long as we're alive, we've still got ample loving to say, be, and do. The Infinite One, "everlasting love," needs us earthlings to suit up and contribute as determined and productive teammates.

So, we home-stretchers lovingly advance, and we lovingly fall. Sometimes we will tumble forwards and other times backwards. Yet "an ever-evolving love" remains our first and final earthly mission.

Making Peace with Our Own Death

CHAPTER FOUR

Preparing for Our Own Farewell

The readiness is all.
—WILLIAM SHAKESPEARE, *HAMLET*

My pastoral experience reveals that too many of us are waiting around to die rather than getting ready to die. The distinction matters. Instead of sputtering or coasting, we would be better off: animating our specks of stardust, mustering intentional goodbyes, making amends, and "packing all our bags" as Pope John XXIII urged—in short, summing up before shuffling off. I've chosen to muse upon my transience and forthcoming expiration, right here and now, plotting (and plodding) the best I can and conveying soulful lessons while still conscious.

Traveling in Zimbabwe, Africa in the mid-1990s, Carolyn and I came across a keen proverb that remains fastened to my heart: "It's important that when death finds you, it finds you alive!" Truly, when we come to die, we need to have our spiritual houses fairly clean and in respectable shape. We need to stay wakeful, not knowing precisely when we'll stop breathing.

When poet and troubadour, Rev. Ric Masten, who was suffering from incurable prostate cancer, asked God: "How much more time do I have to live?" he received no specific termination date. Instead, the answer Masten got was the one he needed: "Enough, Ric, enough!" Blessedly, our close friend stayed pretty much on purpose unto he died in the spring of 2008.

There are lots of things we can't control about our concluding laps, but, as long as cognition and willpower allow, we can put our material and relational affairs in suitable order. This section of *Making Peace with Our Own Death* will focus upon twenty-four prominent questions that might be addressed when facing death squarely. I will state each query and offer reflective commentary. Then the work is yours.

I. *What are my favorite words or phrases to describe dying/death?*

"Dubbing" death gets us thinking earnestly and creatively about the topic. During the course of leading *Mindful Dying* workshops, as well as scrutinizing my own thoughts, here are some of the phrases, in no prioritized fashion, that have arisen:

- Last hooray or hurrah

- Final goodbye
- Melting into God
- Going home
- Only darkness
- Crossing the river
- Rest assured
- Fare thee well
- Dissolving
- Tasty to the last drop
- Nothingness
- Off to a better world
- Non-self
- Back to Mother Earth
- Gone
- "Grand Luminosity"
- Shuffling off the mortal coil
- Into the everlasting arms
- Utter emptiness
- Change-of-address
- De-animation
- Heaven
- From dust to dust
- Immutable radiance
- Sayonara

In the workshop, folks are given time to talk about each preference in twos or threes followed by group discussion. Naturally, when we address the latter question: "What happens to us when we die?" there will be more to say.

II. *How am I presently facing the death of loved ones and friends? How am I comforting and companioning them? How am I honoring their wishes?*

Dying is not just a medical event. It's much more about relation-ships.
At the heart of it, all we can really offer each other is our full attention.
When someone is dying, their tolerance for bullshit is minimal.
—Frank Ostaseski

Answering this set of questions not only helps to shape meaningful farewells with others, but also readies us for how we wish to be treated when we ourselves are dying. Here are some of my rumi-nations.

Albert Schweitzer (1875-1965) was an Alsatian polymath who became an honorary member of our Church of the Larger Fellow-ship in 1962. He claimed, and rightly so, that all who felt pangs of suffering belonged to the largest cooperative in the world: "the fellowship of pain." However, belonging to that guild means little, unless we're ready to join the forces of comfort and healing when-ever one of our kin (and that entails every living being) is injured, dying, or grief-stricken.

Comfort literally means "to stand firm alongside one another." It doesn't require us to be miracle workers or full-time custodians and involves no showy or heroic performance. The word "care" has its roots in the old Gothic term *kara*, which means to lament.

The real meaning of care, then, has to do with empathetically experiencing the pain of another and choosing to be as present as mutually desirable. As long as we're alive, we can bring comfort and care to another life—a plant, an animal or a human—that is suffering. Our dear friend and colleague, Richard Gilbert, puts it succinctly: "Caring is our calling, and we're all called."

I concur with Kahlil Gibran who claimed that "great people have two hearts: one bleeds and the other forebears." We need two hearts and would use them as interchangeably as we employ our right and left feet. When friends are ill or dying, they desire us to weep with them amidst pulsating fear and anguish. They also covet companions who can step aside from the suffering and remain sturdy as rocks.

But there's a fine line, isn't there? If our heart turns maudlin and mushy, then we may sentimentalize into irrelevance. On the other hand, if our heart stands faint and detached, it's liable to harden in no time at all. Our task is to keep both hearts ready, on call, for service to our kin, then to know which heart to exercise.

Furthermore, we are all "wounded healers," thus called to be both caregivers and care-receivers. We need to be strong enough to give care and vulnerable enough to receive care. That was certainly the case during our 24-year ministry in San Diego. Carolyn and I lost three of our beloved parents as well as endured other personal and familial crises, and we needed congregants to bring us solace. And they delivered.

Even when we're unable to be cured, let alone, healed, we can be calmed. The wise ones among us understand life to be an ongoing struggle—not an unbearable one, but surely sorrow-laden—until we're released at the time of death. We are fulfilled and make peace with our own mortality through comforting and being comforted. When Baron von Hugel (1852-1925), the prominent Austrian theologian and mystic, lay dying, his niece could see his lips moving but couldn't catch what he said. So, she put her ear close to his mouth and heard the last words that von Hugel ever uttered: "Caring is everything, nothing matters but caring!"

Humaneness requires that we partner our fellow creatures, morn through evening—becoming each other's compassionate companions. But doing so will vary: showing up, making phone calls, remembering in our prayers, singing, writing notes, touching or massaging gently, sitting quietly, or conversing when together. There are manifold ways to be present and stay connected with folks who are suffering and/or dying.

A musical colleague from Glendale, Arizona regularly escorts a small group of singers into hospice care centers. While there, they will sing repetitively, for about ten minutes, Melanie DeMore's exquisite chant (or a comparable one): "We are sending you light, to calm/heal you, to hold you. We are sending you light . . . to hold you in love." No additional words, just choral comfort.

Another ballad I sometimes sing in nursing homes is "Love, Call Me Home"—composed in 2005 by Peggy Seeger (Pete's half-sister)—one verse of which runs:

When the waves are deep, friends, carry me over.
When I cry in my sleep, Love, call me home.
Time, ferry me down the river, friends, carry me safely over,
Love, tend me on my journey. Love, call me home . . .

Another one of our friends soothingly plays her harp when folks are dying.

The dying process defies predictability; it's often confusing, messy, laden with quirks, but this much we know to be true: our dying usually yearns to be communal. The head and heart, hands and heels of innumerable folks are often required and desired. Professionals, family, strangers, and buddies are summoned to carry us on home. Timothy Leary alerts us that "dying is a team sport," and the Rev. Olivia Bareham, founder of *The Sacred Crossings Institute*, affirms:

The time has come to return death to its rightful place in the circle of life. When we know we are going to die we don't need life-support, we need death-support.

For those who don't have family or friends, available or nearby, fret not, for there exist trained "death doulas." Doulas have become end-of-life soul mid-wives, transitional coaches, lending their presence as folks leave this earthly plane. In the past decade, death doulas and death cafes have blossomed to create what's being called "death positivity." Death doulas help usher us home, bringing succor and meaning to our closing daze. Might you be ready or willing to request a doula or become one yourself?

For the past decade I've been blessed to be both a life-room and death-bed crooner in nursing homes. Our spirits may be sagging and dragging, but our moods are elevated whenever we share songs such as "Stand by Me," "Lean on Me," "No One is an Island," The Greatest Love of All," "Put a Little Love in Your Heart," and "What a Wonderful World" which, by the way, was written intentionally as an antidote to the racially-combustible climate of the United States in the 1960's. Despite the torrent of violence sweeping our contemporary society, Louis Armstrong's popular hit of yesteryear still reminds us that it can be "a wonderful world," if every child of God dares to contribute her/his/their fair share to make it more so.

Pete Seeger (1919-2014), premier American folk singer and activist, captured the formidable power of community singing:

Music cannot change the world, but people can, and sometimes music can change people. Songs will never save the planet, but neither will books nor speeches. But songs are sneaky things. They slip across borders and proliferate in prisons. They penetrate hard shells.

Every time I hoist my own guitar to play, I reverberate with the words engraved upon the circumference of Seeger's banjo: "this instrument surrounds hate with love and forces it to surrender!"

I sing in one nursing home where the live-in residents suffer from severe dementia. Some are sleeping, others may be mouthing the words, and more are barely cognizant of my company. Countless people writhe from an unpreventable, incurable, progressive brain disease called Alzheimer's. However, never forget this: the ailing person is no empty shell but is fortified with soul. Even when visitors are not recognized, they may sense who we are; even when the ailing cannot speak, they still possess receptors. While breathing, everyone inhabits a "life-world" beneath and beyond cognition. Love can always be both served and felt.

Just as we all possess a birthright, we also harbor a *deathright*— which means being able to die as we wish, alone or together, quietly or listening to our favorite music. As Kathleen Dowling Singh, Dharma practitioner and author, asserts:

When it is time to help a loved one face death, may we not distract them from the natural process of enlightenment, of dying into grace. May we allow them to turn their attention to the natural order of the universe, to the Center, to Spirit.

So, I ask: what will be your farewell salute to a dying compatriot? Paying respects at the funeral is crucial but too late. Viewing the coffin may occur, but s/he/they is not really there. They won't hear firecrackers or any 21-gun salute. So, stand ready to show up as your buddy is dying and participate in a bedside vigil (if that is what the dying person might wish). Words, tears, touch, song, or silence may be the order of *their* moment. If unsure, just be present and attend lovingly. Always lovingly!

III. *How am I choosing to eulogize friends and loved ones?*

Don't aim for grandiosity; instead pursue the small and telling stroke, the bull's-eye-detail.
—Ron Marasco

Silence may be our best gift to the dying, as a Jewish proverb informs: "the deeper the love, the less tongue it hath." But there is also a time to eulogize the dead whom we esteem. Again, answering this question fittingly prepares the living for how we might wish ourselves to be recalled. Unitarian Universalism insists that every human being is worthy of honorable attention, living or dying. Dead animals and botanical species deserve our deference as well.

When toasting the deceased, we tend to gravitate toward hyperbole, so that mourners barely recognize the body in the casket.

Remember the derivation of the word *eulogy* is "true story." A syrupy, idealized portrait benefits no one. We would be wiser to pay honest and proper homage to each distinctive, never-before, never-again, creature. The dead need not be glorified, only dignified, and mainly, thereafter, by the quality of the lives of the survivors.

We carry forth, in our own character and conduct, our dead dears!

IV. *In my daily life, how am I practicing death: saying goodbye to people, stuff, dreams, skills, memories, and more?*

Lest you think the notion of "practicing dying" is some off-beat concept arising in the 21st century, please note its noble antecedents. The Prophet Mohammed (571-632 A.D.) put it tersely: "Die before you die" and was joined with analogous comments by both Plato (424-348 B.C.), Athenian truth-seeker, and by Montaigne (1533-1592), French Renaissance philosopher.

Plato said that practicing dying every day was a vital human endeavor. Every time we shed material items in our attic or family room, we are practicing dying. When we cut asunder a hurtful memory or an unresolved glitch, we are practicing dying. When we make tolerable peace with a failing function, we are practicing dying. When we release some want or someone daily, we are practicing dying. We are staying in sound spiritual form for our subsequent crossing. We are getting coffin-ready. We are rehearsing for our final exit.

And in the words of Montaigne:

Let us deprive death of its strangeness. Let us frequent it, let us get used to it; let us have nothing more often in mind than death. We do not know where death awaits us, so let us wait for it everywhere. To practice death is to practice freedom.

The final soulful stage in Hinduism is called *Sannyasa* and means "renunciation." In a world of change and impermanence, *Sannyasa* nudges us to let go, let be, and let come . . . rather than clinging to afflictive emotions and compulsive behaviors. We seniors would do well to practice the subtle art of subtraction during our procession toward death. As Lao Tzu (unknown, 6th-4th century B.C.) encourages: "If you want to become full, let yourself be empty."

Ram Dass (1931-2019), psychologist and spiritual teacher, seconds the discipline of renunciation when he offers: "As we practice dying, we are learning to identify less with Ego and more with Soul." For when we die to attachments along the path, we're better prepared to release everything when it comes our turn to stop breathing. We learn that death isn't waiting for us at the end of the road; death's been tracking us along the way.

It's well-nigh impossible to come face-to-face with our own death and expect to relinquish our bodies and minds smoothly unless we've been dropping, day in and day out, minor as well as major belongings, worries, and affections. To get ready for what no one can ever truly prepare for—the possibility of eternal nonbeing—we must daringly venture moments of dying daily.

Sallie Tisdale, in her book *Advice for Future Corpses* (2018), honestly confesses at the outset: "I have never died, so this entire book is a fool's advice. Birth and death are the only human acts we cannot practice." I wish to revise her claim. To be sure, we'll never be able to replicate what actually happens at death, yet all of our pre-death exercises of relinquishment are useful. They groom us for our eventual crossing.

Here is my daily pledge, mid-May, amidst our thundering pandemic: "I will release some want, some wound, some recollection, some wart, or some person . . . this very afternoon."

V. *How am I preparing for my own death?*

Clearly, this book and its attendant workshop course and materials focus chiefly upon personal and spiritual "preparations" to be made in facing one's own death. Nevertheless, I would also urge readers to tackle all outstanding financial, legal, and relational end-of-life matters.

There are ample resources and books written on these issues, so I will solely reference one pivotal document that Carolyn and I have employed: *Five Wishes* (Aging with Dignity, P. O. Box 161, Tallahassee, Florida 32302-1661).

This is a pamphlet primer that gives folks a way to determine how we wish to be treated when seriously ill or preparing for our own deaths, as we're doing here. It was written with the help of the American Bar Association and the nation's leading experts in end-of-life care.

It is trouble-free to use. All you have to do is check a box, circle a directive, or write a few sentences. Here are areas of focus: "the person I want to make care decisions for me when I can't; the kind of medical treatment I want or don't want; how comfortable I want to be; how I want people to treat me; and what I want my loved ones to know."

You sign the *Five Wishes* form, have it witnessed by two people, and notarized, if necessary, in your State. Then you share a copy with a health care agent, your lawyer, as well as with family members and other loved ones. You store the original copy in a special place in your home (remember where it is!), and give your doctor, lawyer, and clergy each a copy. If you are admitted to a hospital or nursing home, you take a copy with you and place it among your current medical records.

Carolyn and I have copies of this *Five Wishes* document safely lodged alongside other end-of-life materials both at home and at our First UU Church office in San Diego. Everyone who participates in my workshops is given a copy for their own usage. When filled out, then the distribution process begins.

One more level of preparedness: assisting the youngsters. The Hopis give their young a "death chant" when they pass into adolescence. It's a phrase they're taught to repeat every day, especially at moments of danger and uncertainty. It is intended to assist them in merging with the Great Spirit when they die.

How are we Unitarian Universalists preparing our children and teenagers for their final fortune? Are we walking graveyards, talking last things, and gracing them with death chants? Have we produced a curriculum like *Our Whole Lives: Lifespan Sexuality Education* on death and dying? Too frequently parents don't wish to burden or worry offspring, and children aren't ready to talk about death. And friends back away. So, the room stands: dead silent.

We can do better than that. We prepare our offspring for school. We prepare them for safe and healthy social, sensual, and sexual interactions. We prepare them for avoiding harm and handling emotional crises. We prepare them for driving vehicles. We prepare them for the job world. How might we best prepare them for dying . . . ours and theirs?

It all starts with adults spending meaningful time with the youngers—our own as well as those beyond our family—while we're awake and vital. Tribal wisdom would gather and call in the elders, seasoned cradlers of the entire village, weighing us with one charge: help bring to spiritual maturation yet another child. We seniors are "soulfully gifted," as a friend puts it, since we've experienced innumerable heartaches and satisfactions. Now is the season to pass our gifts along . . .

You and I will unlikely ever attain the stature of *shaman* (wizened link with the spirit world), *tzaddik* ("righteous one"), *sanyasi* (religious ascetic) or *bodhisattva* (assisting one and all in the quest for enlightenment). An acceptable role is to become embodied elders, precisely where we're planted, as the elder tree has done with its purple berries.

There's a glorious passage in Jewish lore, where Abraham visits his great-grandfather, Shem. The elder gives the younger bread and wine, followed by some counsel:

Abraham, my dear one, if you wish to convert the world to Yahweh, surely a worthy mission, you must give folks both bread and wine, the old must be connected to the new, so both can remain vital. On the one hand, bread is clearly best when it's fresh; on the other hand, the older wine is, the better it becomes.

Shem's right on purpose. In order to create the kind of universe of which every age bracket can be duly proud, bread and wine must be offered in tandem; youngsters and seniors need to join hearts and hands. Generational spanning is time never squandered. My mind is sharper, my soul thicker, and my conscience broader whenever I spend time with children and youth. For love, at base, is spelled T-I-M-E.

Are you familiar with the bumper sticker that reads: "The most radical thing we can do is introduce people to one another?" This is sound wisdom and downright germane for generational bridging. The window of time young and old share in common passes by so quickly, the gulf remains so vast, and the hunger is so profound. We owe one another not so much a piece of our minds (although that's part of the bargain) but rather a huge portion of our energy and our embrace. We owe one another what American journalist, H. L. Mencken (1880-1956), called "a terrible loyalty"—terrible as in urgent and daunting yet enjoyable.

Marc Freedman, CEO of *Encore.org*, has written a recent book called *How to Live Forever: The Enduring Power of Connecting the Generations* which sports an unmistakable thesis: if seniors want to live forever, then we need to spend more quality time with younger folks, swapping notes and hopes. Lamentably, Freedman documents that only 1/3 of all elders exhibit a purpose beyond them.

Our younger ones don't seek glad-handers or short-timers, marshmallows or reflections of themselves. They sorely clamor to be just who they are—children and youth—and they can best be such when we seniors are seniors: distinct yet equal abettors in creating a more just and joyful universe. In intergenerational exchanges of respect and care, we're lighting one another's torches. We're *con-spiring*—literally, "breathing together" more acutely than we could ever breathe alone. And, as an elder, I'm aspiring to plant seeds without being around for the harvest.

There's no pre-pandemic engagement more gratifying during my week than Monday afternoon sessions with Quinn (she/hers—pronouns), a 15-year-old homeschooler whose mother works at our church. Consequently, Quinn spends much of her learning time there, and I'm privileged to be part of Quinn's life-curriculum. We perform magic tricks, sing and play guitar together, and share the good and bad stuff of our respective lives. And, yes, we've even talked about *death* along the way. We call ourselves *Los Dos Amigos*. I rue the day when Quinn will graduate and take-off on her own. Or I die, without our getting to say goodbye to one another. But I've quit squawking because we blessedly enjoy one another for the time being. Departure will come when it comes.

Additionally, one of the most prized and satisfying junkets of my closing days has been singing in another nursing home alongside our 24-year-old grandson, Trevor. We're both guitarists, so we play and sing some of his favorite contemporary pieces as well as my old standards. The residents in this nursing home are suffering severe cognitive decline, so most are seen mouthing the words, nodding, smiling, and snoozing . . . yet invariably with a glimmer in their soul. For months prior to the pandemic, Trevor had been away in Las Vegas piling up hours as an airplane pilot, so I've missed singing with him. And so have the residents! Dorothea was recently sunk in a session-long despond, but, as I was leaving, clarified matters: "Where is he? The young one! Bring him back!"

When young people graduated from our religious education program and traipsed off to work, school, or another village, Carolyn and I would hold exit interviews, asking each of them one basic question: "What do you remember most fondly from your religious growth and learning experiences at First UU?" When pressed, they might articulate some of our stated principles; then specific peers and adults would come into focus; naturally, youth mini-cons and summer camps are recalled as well; but above all else, they cherished the revelry of intergenerational company.

Our high school graduates would talk glowingly about candlelight services, Dr. Martin Luther King, Jr. commemorative parades, Saturday work projects, and community protest gatherings. They would salute our all-church parties, where everybody was free to dance with everybody else. They would simply remember with stunning precision and glee those moments when they-and-we were living out our holy and hearty mission as a beloved community of all ages.

In thinking back upon his life, Elie Wiesel (1928-2016), professor, Nobel laureate, and holocaust survivor noted how he had encountered strange and inspiring teachers who, each in her/his/their own way, gave Wiesel something for his journey: "a phrase, a wink, an enigma. And I was able to continue." Our children covet our phrases, our winks, our enigmas. We covet theirs. We need one another to be able to continue our respective pilgrimages.

I wrap up this decree of generational bridge-building with a passage from Oren Lyons, known as the Onondaga Faithkeeper:

We always keep in mind the Seventh generation to come. It's our job to see that the people coming ahead, the generations still unborn, have a world no worse than ours—and hopefully better.

Although our number of moves and verdicts is shrinking as we grow long-in-the-tooth, decisions remain ever precious, maybe more precious, and so apropos to the well-being of those not yet born. May we wisdom-keepers live-and-die today, as if we're preparing the way for the seventh generation, because we are. We truly are.

VI. *What are my primary fears concerning my own dying/death and how am I presently facing them?*

When we are, death is not come, and when death is come, we are not.
When we can liberate ourselves from our fear of death, we free ourselves to live.
—Epicurus (341-270 B.C.), Greek philosopher

Some folks actually look forward to death, because they anticipate a locale lovelier than their existing residence. Perhaps they've been in too much pain for too long, and death will bring relief at last. Surely, during this current or any ensuing pandemic, there will be people hankering to die out of physical or economic desperation. They're more frightened of staying alive than of dying.

The words *sacred* and *scared* are identical, except for the transposition of one letter. It's a fruitful twist, because when we elders and crones face what scares us, we are treading on sacred ground. Or as the poet Rumi informs:

Our greatest fears are like dragons guarding our greatest treasures.

Fear is often the finger pointing out where the challenge is; going in the direction of fear can push us toward soulful growth. One veteran colleague alerted me, when I was launching my ministry: "Tom, you will definitely need to learn to hug your monsters."

There's a fine line, of course, between bravely facing our angst and taking stupid risks with valuable things, bonds, and time. However, the dragons of elderhood can't be easily ignored, denied, or wished out of existence. They can't be suppressed or seduced. The majority of them must be met.

What Epicurus says about death makes rational sense, except we're incurably anxiety-ridden creatures; hence we remain saddled with one fear or another as we approach death. Each of us possesses distinct fears, plus we will likely exhibit different ones during the process of our dying, our very death itself, and when we're gone.

Here are some of my own fears, as well as those mentioned in our workshop sessions. The dominant qualms regarding the process of dying seem to be: fear of suffering a slow and agonizing death; fear of dying in a state of confusion or distress; fear of winding up all alone; fear of losing what is safe, familiar, loving, and secure; and fear of perishing suddenly or violently in a car crash, shooting, uncontrollable blaze, or a drowning, without having the chance to share any meaningful farewells. Then, there are fears of what happens when we're dead: fear of being sent to hell and languishing in a scorching fire; fear of dying without anyone either waiting for us or remembering us; fear of losing our true identity; and fear of dwelling forever amidst pure silence, darkness, and nothingness.

It's reported that Hindu and Buddhist yogis meditate at graveyards and on cremation grounds to become more intimate with the processes of decay and transformation. Tibetan monks blow ceremonial horns made from human femurs and eat out of bowls carved from humanoid skulls. In these ventures, they're brazenly confronting life-and-death. But such practices fit neither my personality nor my desires. How about you?

The cheeky Tibetan siddha, Milarepa (1052-1135 C.E.), was willing to invite his imagined fears over for an afternoon cup of tea. This yogi bids us to face our worst demons around death and talk things through with them. It certainly can't hurt to do so.

One of my workshop participants, invited by a church friend, paid our overall process a major compliment in her evaluation form: "I'm now less afraid of dying. I'm readier to die. I'm looser, freer, and calmer. Thank you; thank you more than I can say!"

VII. *What grieves me most about leaving this life? What makes me sad or heartbroken? What dies with me when I die?*

Here's a *tanka* poem (an unrhymed Japanese verse form comprised of 5 lines: containing 5, 7, 5, 7, and 7 syllables respectively) that I recently composed on this very concern:

Leaving behind wares
Leaving behind family
Leaving behind pals
Leaving behind memories
Leaving everything behind

As a Universalist, I believe that I will return to the Eternal Love that brought me into existence. So, sadness, more than fear, is the nagging emotion around my death. I'm gloomy when I consider facing an irreversible process and the notion of annihilation. I'm sad because I still enjoy living, at least in my present state. I'm sad that I will never be able to hold again the hands of those I love. I'm sad I won't be able to sing and serve anymore. I'm sad I won't be able to see how our children, grandchildren, and great-grandchildren choose to grow up. And yeh, I'm sad I won't likely be able to see our San Diego Padres ever win the World Series, although during this shortened season they've reached the playoffs!

I admit to being a high-control, clingy kind of person. My nature resembles the Tibetan word for attachment: *d'cha* which means "sticky desire." I have trouble releasing and abandoning stuff and self. I am oft-bedeviled with an egoic insistence on ruling what transpires in my life, thus robbing me of satisfactory peace of mind and moment. Hence, on my lampshade is posted a decisive, personal test—the words of the revered "Mother of Light," Dipa Ma (1911-1989): "Everything is impermanent. When you are dead, nothing is yours."

Jiddu Krishnamurti (1895-1986), the Eastern Indian philosopher, asks: "Do you want to know how to die? Think of the thing you treasure the most and drop it. That is death." I moan whenever I ponder the bond or bonds most treasurable in my existence and see them fade or melt away, before my very eyes and beyond my very grip. Irrevocably gone.

Some months ago, visiting our daughter's tribe in Santa Barbara, I was lounging on their living room couch, while Erin and my wife were interior decorating the space. I would pop up for periodic lifting, but basically, I was basking in their high-spirited chatter, marinating in the unmistakable timbre of each voice that I would sooner or later miss. And that is death.

I confess that given the disastrous state in which we find our globe, there are moments when I'm readier than ever to depart the sorry state of our earth. We are a troubled and troubling globe—burdened with ecological disaster, religious intolerance, virulent racism, pandemics, moral divisiveness, economic inequities, and more. I slump with sorrow, knowing what we've bequeathed our descendants and what they will have to face when our generation dies. I feel both gravely sad and apologetic.

VIII. *What will likely be my main regrets when I die?*

The bitterest tears shed over graves are for words left unsaid and deeds left undone.
—Harriet Beecher Stowe (1811-1896)

We drift from fears and sadness to regrets, a neighboring heartache. Research documents that the greatest regret of those dying is having lived a life others planned for or required of us. We unhappily morphed into second-rate versions of someone or something else rather than evolving to selfhood.

Sometime in our adulthood pilgrimage (the earlier, the better) we wake up to the fact that nothing we've ever owned or accomplished can establish our worthiness. Human value isn't found in dollars or trophies. Life's real purpose lies in living from the core, being intrinsically rather than extrinsically motivated, in navigating what I call the voyage of self-possession. Who we *are* is the Creation's gift to us; who we *become* is our return offering.

The virtue of self-care is distinct from being stuck on one's self.

The extremes of narcissism and neglect are dead-ends. Conversely, self-possession is the mark of being a mature and content creature. Our ego isn't the enemy; it's a critical organ to use. It only becomes a liability when it's bloated or misused. A holistic program mandates taking reasonable care of our mind, body, heart, spirit, soul, and conscience: our total being. In due course, becoming our own best friend reaps permanent physical, emotional, relational, and spiritual benefits for one and all.

Jewish scholars note that Abraham's journey commences with Yahweh urging him to "go forth" (Genesis 12:10), alternately translated as "go to yourself." This same idiom is mentioned only twice in the entire Hebrew canon, once at the start of Abraham's quest, then again at the close of his journey, when Abraham has become a bona fide elder, still trekking in search of self. And lest we forget, this memorable patriarch of the Abrahamic religions (including Judaism, Christianity, and Islam) was reportedly 175 years old when he died.

Authenticity comes from a Greek word meaning "self-doer." To be an authentic person, then, is to become the primary author of our needs and wishes. Of course, self-possession must never be confused with self-absorption. As fully-minted authors, we are not permitted to remain isolates. However, mellow elders choose to be accompanied more by buddies than bosses. We listen to guides but steer clear of gurus.

Integrity has to do with our being integrated, undivided, whole persons. Nearing his death, Rabbi Zusya bewailed:

In the coming world, God will not ask me: "Why were you not Isaiah?" because I am not Isaiah. "Why then do you weep?" inquired his disciples.

Rabbi Zusya sighed as he answered: "It's because God will ask me: 'Why were you not Zusya?' and I must face whether or not I've lived up to the potential that lies within me!"

In my 50 plus years of ministry, I've found such self-distress to ring true all too often for parishioners upon their deathbeds.

Naturally, our lives will be filled with broken dreams, remorseful doubts, and scattered "if-onlys." The key is to minimize them as we move toward our conclusion . . . to bury one or two regrets every week. Various ways exist to do this: we can journal them into oblivion; we can discharge them by bellowing in a safe corner of the backyard; or we can confess them prayerfully to another and to ourselves.

A friend of ours, when she was dying, wanted to clean her slate, so she called an antagonist to her bedside and made an offer: "I want to end by being your friend once again; I refuse to die with a grudge. What do you say?"

They embraced and dissolved in tears.

IX. *What am I still angry about?*

Anger alerts us to the fact that something is missing or gone awry in our life. A steady supply of emotional thunder-and-lightning will keep elders properly fierce and free from the erosion of lethargy.

Strangely, anger is one of the most loving emotions we ever experience. If we don't respect someone, we won't risk strong, let alone negative feelings. Anger-with-heart puts fire into an alliance:

a fire that burns, cleanses, destroys, and even heals in service of relational growth and earthly completion. Apathy, not anger, is the opposite of love, and "an ever-evolving love" is the spiritual path we Unitarian Universalists have chosen.

Nevertheless, seniors often fall prey to the harmful extremes of slow-burning bitterness or all-consuming fury. Suppressed anger can result in insomnia, high blood pressure, fatigue, habitual sarcasm, accident proneness, and gastrointestinal disorders. We home-stretchers incur enough maladies without compounding our condition because of unseemly anger. Therefore, as we suffer bouts of anger in facing our death, here are a few guidelines.

First, the Hasidic aphorism lands on target: "Since I've tamed my anger, I keep it in my pocket. When I need it, I take it out." What someone has called "the gift of intelligent rage" can contribute to soulful maturity. I personally hope to stay suitably defiant my whole jaunt homeward. I've just got to remember in which pocket I've placed my anger!

Second, display anger for impact rather than injury, as a psychologist counseled early in my adult formation. Express anger without attacking the other person's ego. Not easy, to be sure, but easy is merely another name for withdrawal, revenge, or compliance. Those who are angry must stick close enough to resolve arguments and grow love. With ingenuity and persistence, we can develop ways to be *angry together.*

Third, partnerships are warned: "Don't go to bed angry." I would add: don't go to your death angry. Is there some ire or vitriol lingering in your system that could be healthfully released? If so, vent said anger and when sufficiently restored, move ahead toward your date with death.

X. *Am I weeping enough before I die?*

Don't get me to hope just yet;
let me abide for a while with
my Holy Lamentation.
—Jonipher Kwong

Taboo after taboo has toppled in modern life, but grieving well remains an obstacle. When ministering to the dying, we know this to be true: comparisons are odious; sweet talk and textbook prayers fall short; and teddy bears only cart so much fluff in the face of the unbearable. *Gref* comes from Middle English meaning "heavy." The word grief and "gravity" and "grave" are etymological kin. Grief entails weight, robbery, loss. It must be confronted rather than denied. Grief cannot be normalized or light-heartened away, only companioned and expressed.

During our devastating global pandemic, I was recently singing to myself, "We are the World," the immensely successful 1985 ballad that raised millions of dollars in humanitarian aid to Africa—and I broke down sobbing. If truth be told, singing regularly brings me to waterworks, whether alone or in nursing homes.

One of my favorite scriptural passages comes from the Upanishads (VII. 23):

That which is Whole is joy.
There is no joy in fractioned existence.
Only the whole is joy.
But one must desire to understand the Whole.

We elders know well, from life-long experience, that the road to joy sometimes goes through the valley of melancholy rather than through the gateway of pleasure. Experts often describe jazz as a mixture of swing and sorrow. Authentic spirituality doesn't attempt to cure sadness, but helps us to live more realistically and gracefully with the blues: both ours and others.

We will mourn broken pledges, tortured bonds, devastated dreams, violated women, abused children, fallen men, harmed animals, and ravaged earth. Our lives to be full and rounded, must marinate periodically in the juices of travail. Sadness is a primal, ontological condition. However, it's not the same state as depression which signals that one is mired in self-denigration and despond and likely needs social and medical assistance. Sadness is irremovable. Depression can be lessened, sometimes eliminated.

Tears and cheers are intertwined during the sweep of our journeys. Vietnamese Buddhist teacher Thich Nhat Hanh regularly uses the expressions "joyful sorrow" and "sorrowful joy." Indeed, healthy home-stretchers are *schmerzenreich*, as the German word evokes—rich in our ability to contain not erase sorrow. "Only the whole is joy."

The day my father died, I remember turning the 1987 Christmas Eve services completely over to Rev. Carolyn, being hugged by our oldest child, then jumping in the car and driving from San Diego to Los Angeles. While motoring, I spilled forth in unchecked tears, memories, and song fragments, sodden in a sweep of emotions that my father's life-and-death evoked. I don't recall; I may have said some words out loud, but no formal prayer was made. I was sighing and groaning, swimming in an ocean of "the feelings that prompt prayer." I had just lost my one and only Dad. Understandably, our personal losses—divorces, deaths, and disappointments—are magnified during the holiday interval of supposed whoopee and wassail. Indeed, no Christmas season arrives now without my feeling the combination of irrevocable joy and bone-deep sorrow. Unfailingly, I huddle close amid loved ones, sing lustily, and weep quietly during the dark, dank, demanding days of December.

Another verity of our personal and professional lives: whenever we fully grieve, we can be comforted. Genuine love knows both anguish and angst. Sufi poet and storyteller Doug von Koss has vowed that whenever tears come, he will let them wet his cheeks, and then allow them to tumble, unwiped, to the ground, so that something might be fertilized and sprout.

One evening Buddha heard wailing in a house he was passing and, upon entering inconspicuously, Buddha found that the householder had died, and her family and neighbors were weeping. Immediately, Buddha sat down and began crying too. An elderly gentleman, shaken by this show of distress in such an illustrious guru, kvetched: "I would have thought that you, the Buddha, were beyond such emotional outbursts!" "On the contrary, it's precisely this crying that helps me through it," Buddha replied through his sobs. The older I get and the closer to death I come, the more I weep as well. Such catharsis can lead to cleansing and comfort. So, I hope, so I pray, so I cry.

In the Christian Scriptures, it is reported: "And Jesus wept." This may be the shortest verse in the bible, but what a colossal phrase. The Nazarene was distraught over the rotten behavior of his people and instead of ranting and railing, drafting an oration, or marshaling forces to mount some political retaliation; he was simply moved to tears. Sometimes falling to pieces is the only way to pull ourselves back together again.

We Americans, especially men, are notorious for trying to tough things out. Our problem is too little bawling for our own good. The cost to our health is often enormous, as one physician states: "Sorrows that find no vent in tears may soon make our organs weep." We cry because we love and throb, sting and care. The wetter, the better. Believe me, there are tears galore in my *Mindful Dying* workshops. We let the tide gush from every corner of every eye in the room.

One participant presently suffers pulsating pain throughout her whole being: digestive problems and degenerating limbs, plus her mind is slipping out of range. At root, the word suffering means "to feel sharply;" and that's what is happening throughout Rosie's body and psyche. She is now into bargaining with God, over her stricken state: "Okay God, I'll somehow make it through this mess, on the road to death; but it counts as my worst one, right?" Well, to be honest, I'm not so sure it does, for Rosie appears caught in a precipitous plunge. Sometimes, we depart throbbing.

Naturally, it helps to recognize that we don't own our bodies; we only have them on loan. Yet, it's quite another—more complicated, even shameful—reality, when we can't control our own bodies. Painful queries haunt us and those who love us: who's going to be around to cut our dirty and gnarled toenails? Who will be long-suffering with our cognitive lapses, hobbled hips, and incontinence? And who will take care of us when the competence, the patience, even the love of family members or friends per chance wears thin, even out? It's one thing to suffer philosophically; it's another to slip, slip, and slip away . . . becoming a load, if not a burden, to others. Sometimes our lives are completely whacked. Under such conditions, it's dreadfully difficult to finish well. One request dominates: "O God . . . just let me go, quickly!"

So, what can we possibly do as Rosie's fellow comforters? Well, good grief counselors, such as Stephen and Ondrea Levine, would encourage embattled seniors to attend to our own pain as if we were tenderly soothing a child, holding it in a calming embrace. We're advised to breathe softly into the direct seat of our hurt, repeating a mantra such as: "Eternal Spirit of Life and Love: fill my body and soul with healing kindness." Taking long and leisurely breaths has been known to assist the soul, no matter the state of our body. To accompany each inhalation and exhalation with monosyllabic words such as in and out, slow and deep, thanks and yes, smile and rest, heal and peace, can produce a palliative place in the midst of intense suffering. Sometimes, these rituals help; other times, they fall short. No guarantees.

Confucius wept, when he understood that he would soon die. We too will likely weep upon the appearance of the Grim Reaper—hopefully, tears of sorrow and joy, gratitude and hope. Facing death squarely, may you and I welcome a good mourning.

XI. *Have I composed a Life-Review?*

You matter because you are,
and you matter to the end of your life.
—Dame Cecily Saunders, founder of
the Hospice Movement, 1960

Later on we will work on biographical sketches for our own memorial services. This is an early effort to address some major themes of our specific journey. Some call it a Life-Review, others an Odyssey or a Spiritual Geography. Obviously, we could engage in an invaluable series of exercises just documenting the story of our existence, but we're inviting the creation of a mere summary here. Some people find it helpful to sketch a timeline from birth until now with dates marking significant personal passages.

(1) What are the most defining *moments* or *turning points* of your life? Give each a title and paragraph of description.

(2) What are the most nourishing and joyful *relationships* of your life? Give each a title and a complete paragraph.

(3) What have been the most difficult times and/or unresolved *issues* of your life? Again, give each a heading, hew a paragraph, and then name the lesson learned from each challenge.

(4) What *challenges* lie ahead for you—spiritual invitations awaiting your personal response? Describe them in fitting detail.

(5) Compose a short *epitaph* (50 words or less) that captures the heart of your character and conduct. Or craft what's termed a personal "six-word *memoir*." The latter doesn't have to be a complete sentence and can contain unrelated terms, but it focuses upon one central theme. If one such memoir doesn't suffice, script several.

Here are a few that I've fashioned in *Mindful Dying* workshops: "loved, he gambled living on love;" "aspired to be daring, caring, sharing;" and "struggled mightily to major in kindness." Then there's what's called the "*tombstone test*," wherein you write your name, date of birth, scribble a substantial dash, predict the imagined year (maybe, even the day) of your death, then produce a personal phrase you'd like scrawled on your gravestone. When the younger generations join my classes, you're more likely to see a bodily inscription or "tattoo."

Awhile back, I was feebly trying to encapsulate the substance of a parish friend during her memorial tribute. In case you didn't know it, we ministers occasionally stumble our way through such passages. Surprisingly, the spirit stirred, and I sputtered forth something like: "Marlene knew how to light fires in cold rooms!" Whoops, I used a nine-word memoir for her, but you get the point.

Throughout this process, I encourage folks to brag some about themselves. Sample tombstone phrases have included: "carrier of joy;" "shameless agitator;" "bridge-builder;" "plodder to the end;" "champion of liberty;" so forth and so on. Each of us exudes different and positive qualities. We will be recalled, after we die, from the vantage point of others. This is our own clear-cut "shot" prior to our deaths.

Then as comfortable, participants are asked to share self-portrayals with others in the sacred circle. We may also take our Life-Review material home and keep revisiting and refining our sketches as often as the spirit invites.

This exercise is primarily for our own personal benefit, but we may choose to disclose the content with family members and friends. Or we may wish to keep it hidden in a file to be revealed only after we die. Or we may decide to write it; then dispose of it.

Here's another pointer to consider in composing our Life-Reviews. It comes via the perceptiveness of American writer E. B. White (1899-1985):

I arise in the morning torn between a desire to improve (or save) the world and a desire to enjoy (or savor) the world. This makes it hard to plan the day.

White conveys a conundrum. However, at our finest, we humans balance both experiences of savoring and moments of service, all the way to our benediction. As colleague Jaco ten Hove declares: "We Unitarian Universalists aspire to be 'both-and-ians." Or as my tennis buddy would always drive home: "Tom, never forget that there's a yin and a yang to every *thang!*"

I've always admired the Nobel Prize winner Linus Pauling (1901-1994), a scientist and peace activist who was also a committed Unitarian Universalist. Pauling acted with propriety and grace in being invited to a White House dinner dance. He spent the day picketing the White House in opposition to American nuclear policy. Then he changed into a dinner jacket and spent the evening as the late President Kennedy's guest. Pauling was a person with a sense of proportion and balance. He was an indisputable "both-and-ian!"

XII. *How is my life summing up?*

*I don't want to get to the end of my life
and find that I have lived just the length of it.
I want to have lived the width of it, as well.*
—Diane Ackerman

"Simplify, simplify, simplify" is one of Unitarian Transcendentalist Henry David Thoreau's enduring refrains. It is easy to forget that Thoreau's sojourn at Walden Pond was a more carefree existence than most. He was without partner or children, used rent-free space from the Emerson's to build his cabin, and walked regularly back to Concord to enjoy his friend's company and his mother's vittles. Nonetheless, Thoreau aspired to practice an essential existence. He abided by "higher laws" that enabled him to focus not on livelihood so much as on life itself. His embodiment of the Spartan life remains relevant today, especially for elders and crones advancing homeward.

As our physical strength and mental clarity fade, our world contracts around us. Some of the diminishments are inescapable and externally imposed; others are purposely selected for the sake of cleanup. The afternoon of existence is a most favorable time to update our intimacies, place our personal and spiritual affairs in order, and mull over our lasting legacy—in short, to make adequate peace with who we've been and what we've done during our earthly stint.

I find the queries in the *Creative Sage-ing* workshops led by Jewish theologian Zalman Schacter-Shalomi both illuminating and useful:

Make up a bill of fare for the rest of your life. What do I have appetite for?

What do I want to taste again? What do I want to enjoy for the first time?

What do I not choose to stomach any longer? What would be a healthy diet for living the remainder of my days?

Participants are encouraged to be brutally honest in designing their homestretch menus.

In the process of summation, we would do well to heed the practice of Tibetan Buddhists who begin and complete every daily endeavor—be it eating, writing, cleaning the house, playing, working, meditating, or visiting the sick—with ritual words such as: "I dedicate this activity to my own spiritual awakening so that I may better awaken all beings."

"Generativity versus stagnation" is one of German-American psychoanalyst Erik Erikson's (1902-1994) stages of psycho-spiritual development. Being a *generative* person during our final stretch is equivalent to being a generous person. Love triumphs only if we keep our gifts moving until our body expires, is buried, and buds a subsequent blush of growth. Sooner or later, we recognize that a full existence is not so much about duration as donation. Paying back and paying forward, as they say.

There is an epitaph on an English gravestone that goes to the hub of the magnanimous spirit. "What I kept, I lost. What I spent, I had. What I gave, I have." Without a doubt, when our lives come to a final reckoning, we mostly resemble our gifts of time, talent, and treasure—gifts born of overflowing joy and thankfulness. When all is said and done, we possess nothing except what we have shared or given away. We are the sum of our gifts.

Seniors are invited to row a lighter boat, packed only with necessary cargo. What do I really wish to hold on to and what am I willing to relinquish? Which of my personal effects can be passed on to others, now, while I'm self-governing? How might this spring-cleaning feed my spirit? What are the obstacles to living the conclusion I desire?

Becoming a skillful shedder entails not only thinning out toys, appliances, photos, wardrobe, books, junk, albums, and antiques, but also forsaking pointless routines, nasty manias, and sabotaging grudges . . . getting spiritually ship-shape so that we might dwell at peace with what's left—what we possess, where we live, and who we are—as death draws nigh. I resonate with the lyrical musing of the Spanish poet, Antonio Machado (1875-1939):

And when the day arrives for the final voyage
and the ship of no return is set to sail,
you will find me aboard, traveling light,
almost naked, like the children of the sea.

Some will enjoy short stints on earth, some medium length spells, and some long-term jaunts, yet the same kismet awaits all: we arrive naked, we clothe ourselves, and then we depart stripped and bare.

Countless senior citizens live with clutter that pleads to be dumped, at least pared. We basically need to shed everything that keeps us from being whole during our climb or decline toward death.

Beneficial shedding requires that our eldering vision rotates between that of the *eagle*—seeing the overall landscape from a distance—and the *mouse*—experiencing life's detail up close, at ground level.

However, it's not trouble-free for all seniors, as we come to grips with our downward spiral. Nicholas is a packrat and feels that everything he owns is an integral part of his identity. When pressed, in our workshop, to consider pruning things, Nicholas testily defended: "How dare you denude me of my hard-earned stuff? Don't even suggest it!"

Hallie, who remains less tied to her possessions, is still hassled by the possibility of having to divest herself of decades' worth of things. Hallie doesn't want to burden her life-partner, Louisa, with an overwhelming task when she dies. Nonetheless, at the age of 81, Hallie hardly knows where to start shedding. Hallie and Louisa have scheduled a summit meeting to address this niggling predicament.

When we last conversed, Hallie reminded me of the poignant scene in the movie *Amadeus* that occurs right after a chamber recital, when Mozart is approached by his royal patron and paid a backhanded compliment. The benefactor is quite stirred by the awesome concert, yet feels compelled to offer a modest critique, claiming that this major recital piece seemed to contain "too many notes." Mozart swiftly retorted: "Well, then, which ones, your Excellency, would you have me remove?" That's the quandary posed by death-facing folks as well: Which of my prized household possessions would you have me discard? And how can I reduce and crop in a manner that makes for a pleasurable discipline rather than another loathsome chore?

There's no uniform or easy answer to this thorny issue, but here's one suggested path for sifting memories and shedding objects. Whether living alone or in a partnership, I invite you to walk around your dwelling by yourself. Bask in the reminiscences. It may take months or longer before you're convinced to keep something, pass it onto loved ones, give it to a thrift shop or rummage sale, or cart it to the dumpster. There will always be private possessions left over for the bereaved to handle after we die, but they should be kept to a manageable minimum. Remember one objective of making peace with our death is to bless, not saddle, others.

Carolyn and I are summing up in slightly distinct ways. She has photographed most of her/our precious keepsakes and written notes under the photos describing the story behind each item. Then each of our children, when we both are dead, will be able (hopefully, in a fair and agreeable manner) to select which ones they cherish. She's also currently dispensing a few objects, so our family's joy might be maximized. On the other hand, I've written notes about my valued memorabilia in my proverbial *Green* ("Go, Go, Go Do It!") *Book*: the repository of other end-of-life directives and miscellany as well. Therein, I offer some specific gift-links to each child and grandchild. No photos. I'm also distributing things right now, lighting our respective hearts aglow.

Our life-summation demands even more from our souls. I heartily endorse the sentiment of Paul in Romans 13:8:

Owe no one anything, except to love one another.

As we elders approach our death, tapering everything we possess down to *love* itself is the consummate discipline. We are roused to plow meticulously through our closets, cupboards, files, accounts, and odds and ends. We can take our time, no rush, because we're still cogent and in charge. To whom might we owe money, a conciliatory word, clothes, a photograph, crystal, or artifacts? Perhaps we owe an overdue embrace or a moldy, yet meaningful, volume. And how about owing a word of hope? If so, whenever possible, I nudge us to deliver, all of the above, personally.

Our aim: reckon up and leave life . . . debt-free and love-filled.

Here's another practice. Many native cultures measure wealth not by what we possess but by what we're able to hand on. They celebrate *potlach*, or the great giveaway, where objects are liberally distributed to the neediest in the greater community. We're doing that as well, in our household—usually giving material items to the homeless center I co-founded in 1984 and where I currently volunteer. This mode of *potlach* is particularly meaningful, when I view clients walking off with my donated apparel.

Ultimately, there will be our last *potlach*: the giving away of our entire corpus back to the earth from whence we came. Other animals do it. Buffaloes bestow all their parts—flesh, hide, and horns—for the benefit of kindred. Trees compost the soil. An ever-evolving love summons all of us two-leggeds to sow, plant, and harvest, then give away the bounty of our being upon death.

Here's another way to reflect upon "spilling out our treasure," based on a piece from May Sarton (1912-1995), prolific Belgian-American poet who felt a strong affinity for Unitarian Universalists who continue to venerate her work:

I would like to believe when I die that I have given myself away like a tree that sows seeds every spring and never counts the loss, because it is not a loss, it is adding to future life . . . strongly rooted, perhaps, but spilling out its treasure on the wind.

I confess to relishing the hope that my death might "add to future life." That's my plan and wish, spilling out whatever treasures

I might either own or embody back to the earth as well as into the hearts of future generations.

Just prior to our 95-year-old mother moving into a nursing home for the final month of her life, she sat in a favorite chair in the middle of her duplex living room. Surrounded by her two sons, our mates, and some grandchildren, as well as one close friend, Mary Catherine Flanagan Towle dispersed items of personal value such as a piano, a bookcase, silverware, ceramic vases, clothes, and furniture—even her engagement ring. Books had already been parceled out, mainly to her church library.

Mom was cogent enough to relish the gifting of her modest number of heirlooms, occasionally selecting the recipient and at other times just allowing the choices to flow. Throughout the process, she held sway. Everyone received something of worth and felt personally graced. When a snafu occurred, we two sons conferred and made the call. Overall, it was an intimate gathering that brought serenity and gladness to both our nonagenarian mother as well as her devoted survivors.

Futile dreams and festering emotions need to be shorn as well. Summation has everything to do with interior mop-up—releasing obsolete and spiteful thoughts—a crucial route to authentic en-*lighten*-ment. The sunset of our existence is arguably the prime season to ruminate, prune, and select what remains worthy of our humanity.

Nevertheless, we'll continue to make bum decisions and disappoint folks, all the way home, so there exist perennial needs to forgive and be forgiven. We need to stay keen and caring of spirit right up until we die. Louise Penny puts it affectingly:

Avoid spiritual Alzheimer's: the incremental loss of the ability to be grateful and joyful about the daily gifts of life, no matter what the circumstances of our lives are at that moment.

So true! We seniors tend to fixate upon bodily decline and notice eroding mental capacity, while forgetting to stem the tide of our potential, oft progressive, spiritual lapses.

XIII.   *Am I ready to reckon with my own evil?*
Both the capacity for brutality and the capacity for love exist in all of our hearts. A belief in our innocence is not an option. We must find a place that can know the reality of both.
—William Sinkford

Unitarian Universalists have been soft on sin and evasive with evil. Our historical emphasis has been upon the human potentiality for good, even our perfectibility. We've been riveted on the progress of the human race, "onward and upward forever." We've all sinned and continue to do so, and our sins come in various shapes and sizes. And they're more than just personal peccadilloes. Sin also involves collective and transgenerational irresponsibility: war, economic injustice, sexual orientation bigotry, racial oppression, colonialization, gender violence, environmental degradation, and more—such sins don't only break rules; they destroy people and devastate earth.

Look at our Source II: "Words and deeds of prophetic women and men which call us to confront powers and structures of evil with justice, compassion, and the transforming power of love." One of our major Unitarian Universalist flaws is our rush to handle evil as if it were solely an external reality while failing to admit our own sins and wrongdoings, both as a progressive movement and as well-intentioned individuals.

For example: Selma, 1965. We were rightly combating the racial injustices embodied in the Jim Crow system and southern white supremacy of that era, while essentially ignoring, certainly minimizing, our own ingrained white entitlements and biases as an Association, which continue to this day. Substantive and unwavering justice always starts with cleaning up one's own residence and knowing full well that the work is never done.

Our reluctance as a "liberal religion" to admit, let alone fully stem, our grievous history of clergy sexual misconduct is another example . . . demonstrated early in my own ministry. I was your "golden boy" aspiring to eradicate the evils of the world, while being good and looking good. Then I committed a shameful wrong in breaking my marital vow and leaving my marriage to partner with Carolyn, a member of my congregation. I performed an evil act. I transgressed.

On the one hand, marrying Carolyn was the right choice. On the other hand, leaving my marriage was an act of personal, relational, and ministerial misconduct. I hurt and harmed my wife, another spouse, my daughter and Carolyn's children, friends and other family members, my church, my colleagues and my profession . . . the list is lengthy. To this day, I'm still wrestling with the consequences of this difficult and damaging decision. My ministry has become a checkered exercise in forgiving and being forgiven, in confessing my past wrongdoing while forging a worthy present, in raising a phoenix from the ashes.

I have cast my lot with a realistic yet buoyant faith, a resilient and hopeful religion. I truly believe people can change, atone, and become stronger precisely where we have wounded others or been wounded by them. However, such regeneration doesn't come easily, without a cost and substantial accountability. Real, lasting transformation demands repentance and restitution. *Semper reformanda.*

What I recall most about being grilled in 1970 before the UU Ministerial Fellowship Committee in Seattle was being stopped cold by the Rev. Dr. Paul Carnes' stern yet germane question: "Well, Tom, you seem like a capable, good enough guy. But how does your theology deal with evil, more explicitly with your own evil?" Despite fumbling forth some feeble response at the time, I made it inside our fold. But I've been occupied with that question ever since. My entire ministry has been a steadfast, sometimes spineless, effort to "love the hell" out of my own soul, much less that of society.

I'm sharing this ministerial confession forthrightly in my final book, not only for abetting my own restoration, but also as a goad for each participant in the *Mindful Dying* process to undertake a comparable process of recognition and atonement.

There exists a deep driving desire in human nature to become a morally responsible being. In the end, we want to confess, be judged, then, whenever possible, to compensate and be forgiven. We want to stand accountable in the face of death: as a person, as a partner, as a parent, as a patriot, and as a religious pilgrim. We seek some sort of reckoning, a time of assessing the character and conduct of our days. Approaching our own death is the ideal time to do this . . . our final chance.

Indeed, the older I get, the more I value authentic confession. It can be cathartic and liberating to voice my offense, out loud and directly, either to the aggrieved person or to an impartial and supportive listener. Despite confessing to a therapeutic other, our sense of sin needs to be dealt with in the private courts of our inner domain, before any significant renewal can be navigated. We need to own our evil, as reported in the Prodigal Son parable "when he came unto himself." So, I challenge liberals to take another look at the concept of repentance, the bridge between sin and redemption. It's a noble word and a worthwhile process. Repentance doesn't mean breast-beating or wallowing in guilt or shame. It literally means to stop what we're doing, turn around, change directions, make reparations, and get back on course. In the parlance of 12 step recovery groups: repentance entails taking a fearless moral inventory, admitting where we're wrong, and making amends whenever possible. As Ezekiel (18:31) observes: repentance can lead to our possessing "a new heart and a new spirit." Our Association, our country, and our world need "a new heart and a new spirit." So do you and so do I.

Unitarian Universalist minister Suzanne Meyer aptly expresses it:

Such is the real meaning of repentance: not trying to blame bad genes, bad parents, or bad role models, or the environment factors, but owning up to the fact that you made a wrong turn and are in need of a moral course correction. The objective of repentance is wholeness, reconciliation, and reunion. Repentance in the end is all about taking the most direct way home.

It is never too late to take "the most direct way home."

XIV. *Am I heeding Micah's mandate during my homestretch?*

What does the Eternal require of you, but to do justice,
and to love kindness, and to walk humbly with your God?
—Micah 6:8

The book of the prophet Micah in Hebrew Scriptures denotes a watershed in the evolution of religion when we moved from animal sacrifice to human service and from ritual worship to social righteousness. If one honors Micah's three imperatives of justice, kindness, and humility, then our houses—both personal and institutional—will stand in good order.

Micah contends that these moral demands appear from beyond our ego or imagination. They come from the Eternal, from God, from "everlasting love," from the Creation. They're not intriguing, optional challenges we humans dreamed up. They comprise what is expected—make that *required*—during our adventure from birth until death.

The first imperative is "to do justice." Not to think or visualize justice but to perform justice every waking moment of our lives, not merely when we feel like it. Minor or major deeds will suffice. Private and public actions will qualify . . . even when our lives are nearing completion. Our behavior will always reveal our beliefs.

When I think of justice, my heart revisits 1965 Selma: the spirit, the solidarity, and the sacrifices. We were enmeshed, during this historic March, in what civil rights leader, John Lewis (1940-2020) labelled: "good, necessary trouble." In 2020, both personally and societally, we white elders reside but one gesture, one lapse, one word, one moment of silence, or one deed away from intensifying racism in America. We must remain on duty as moral lieutenants to sustain the courageous struggle of "liberty and justice for all" so tellingly embodied by both Rev. C. T. Vivian (1924-2020) and Congressperson Lewis. Our marching orders are abundantly clear!

I hope to be engaged in righteous tussles for the rest of my life, amidst inevitable breakthroughs and breakdowns. As the glorious spiritual exhorts: "I know one thing we did right . . . was the day we started to fight. Keep your eyes on the prize, hold on, hold on . . ." To fight for equitable change, to scrap and scrape for what's fully just at home and work, in our congregations and in society, always remembering that the nonviolence of Dr. King was neither passive nor weak-kneed but tough-minded and tender-hearted.

Justice entails mending a broken world by making sure that what belongs to people and other animals gets to them: be it freedom, dignity, or resources. The Rev. Rosemary Bray McNatt, current president of Starr King School for the Ministry, challenges us to become unfaltering justice-makers:

The truth is this: if there is no justice, there will be no peace. We can read Thoreau and Emerson to one another, quote Rilke and Alice Walker and Howard Thurman, and think good and noble thoughts about ourselves. But if we cannot bring justice into the small circle of our own individual lives, we cannot hope to bring justice to the world. And if we do not bring justice to the world, none of us is safe and none of us will survive. Nothing that Unitarian Universalists need to do is more important than making justice real—here, where we are.

What does God require of us but to do justice, then "to love kindness?" *Hesed* or steadfast love is mentioned 245 times in the Hebrew Scriptures, denoting both an essential part of God's character as well as the core of our human assignment. *Hesed* isn't a mere feeling or emotion; it indicates compassionate behavior. Furthermore, this second prerequisite is not only to show but also to *love* kindness, which is summed up in one admirable and mighty duty: *lovingkindness.*

One more distinction: kindness is not equivalent to niceness. I believe in being polite and civil, but too much courtesy can degenerate into faintheartedness. There are moments when we should assert rather than defer, intervene and push back rather than submit. Kindness is, first and last, a rugged and stout virtue.

When my days seem spiritually desolate, I resort to chanting #1031 in our hymnal—*Filled with Loving Kindness*—composed by Rev. Ian Riddell (1968—) and based upon the traditional Buddhist *metta.* The words and melody breed quietude in my soul.

May I be filled with lovingkindness.
May I be well.
May I be filled with lovingkindness.
May I be well.
May I be peaceful and at ease.
May I be whole.

Then a second time with "may you" and completed with "may we."

That's the consummate goal of social justice: being kind. When in doubt, be kind; when frightened, risk kindness; when bitter, speak kindly. The English philosopher and mystical universalist,

Aldous Huxley (1894-1963), struck gold when he penned:
> *It's a bit embarrassing to have been concerned with the human problem all one's life and find at the end that one has no more to offer by the way of advice than this—*
>> *"Try to be a little kinder."*

Kindness dwells at the center of Universalist doctrine where radical hospitality triumphs. I'm reminded of the words of our colleague, Charles A. Howe, who wrote:
> *By preaching and practicing kindness, we're at least making a good start on what John Murray was urging people to do (in his 1770 sermon). Who knows? Kindness may take us further than we think!*

Indeed, kindness always does. Think of this second obligation of Micah in terms of our local congregations. Regardless of how open-minded any of our parishes may appear on paper, we're invariably leaving someone out of our spiritual circle. In a sincere effort to broaden our horizons and embrace, we must regularly take stock: Who's missing in our sanctuary? Who's not here but may want to be? What perspective or identity has trouble being seen or heard in our domicile? Then the job of kindness is to find ways to invite the missing ones into our fellowship, if they so wish to join us.

Unitarian Universalism aspires to be a home for all souls, a religion gracious and kind enough to enfold every last creature. Then we swear to observe the admonition of colleague, Barbara Pescan: "After you enter the doors of our faith, you may not lock them after yourself!" How difficult, how extremely difficult, it is to keep the doors of one's own heart . . . as well as the doors of one's family, faith, and world wide-open to ever-evolving justice and kindness.

Here's an example from my volunteering at our local Uptown Inter-faith Service Center for the homeless. One morning, a familiar client (we'll call him Mike) came in, and we got to talking, and before you knew it, I had taken Mike aside and brazenly asked him: "What keeps you going, my friend?" and Mike quickly responded: "H. O. P. E. which stands for *Healthy Options Practiced Every day.*"

I have no idea where Mike got that mantra, but it has stuck with me as a usable prescription for living-and-dying as hopefully as possible. Even though Mike often falls short of its goal; this phrase, he said, keeps him stretching, step by step by step. "Passion for the possible" is Mike's aspiration while not always his achievement. Obviously, the same stands true for me and for you.

Ever since that grace moment, I've used Mike's acronym in my service efforts, especially with children and youth-at-risk. For example, when I first volunteered at a shelter for homeless youth (13-17-year olds, primarily LGBTQIA+ youth), I described our afternoon session as "Hands on Play Every day." Our weekly play shop has involved sharing affirmations, performing meditation exercises, creating magic tricks, crafting collages, talking together, and often has ended with a group chant. This hour of fun has revolved around what I call the 4-Hs: our heads, hearts, hands, and heels summarized in one more H: hustle. And always grounded in the H of all H's: *hope.*

Our hour of H. O. P. E. often has furnished tangible take-a-ways for each youth's backpack (what I labelled their "bag of portable joy"). I'll never forget one young man, at an early session, immediately challenging me: "Yeh, yeh, yeh . . . H. O. P. E. is a hell of a lot better than D. O. P. E.—Dead or Prison Eventually! So, I guess, your job, Mr. Tom, is to help me change from being a hopeless doper to being a dopeless hoper, right? Are you up to it or are you going to quit on me, like most adults I've met?" I struggled, and he struggled, alongside one another, for a couple more months, until he disappeared one night. Unquestionably, hope is locked in a mulish, oft-merciless battle with despair for the souls of every living being, including the younger compatriots extending behind us.

Here's another illustration of desiring to heed Micah's mandate. One of the just and kind covenants we often exhibit at Uptown is having clients, in appropriate situations, serve the Center in return. Hence, you will observe regulars sweeping the patio, lugging crates of food, cleaning the bathroom, sorting clothes, or assisting newer folks in navigating the tricky passage toward possibly garnering shelter or work—helping fellow homeless take an exit off the highway from drugs, violence, or poverty.

One morning, Clyde came to the desk and said: "I believe in reciprocity" and proceeded to slowly and confidently spell out each letter of the word: "R-E-C-I-P-R-O-C-I-T-Y. You gave me some food and clothing yesterday. What is there for me to do at the Center today? It's my turn to help others!" Most of our volunteers are elders with bad knees and balky backs, so we eagerly invited Clyde to do some "heavy lifting" around the Center. He thanked us for the privilege and pleasure of being a reciprocal partner at Uptown. Since that pivotal moment, Clyde has returned regularly, both for services *and* opportunities to serve.

At our best, we earthlings are trying to build a "dignitarian world" as one associate describes it, and to do so, we must regard one another as service-partners. Down-deep, every human wishes to be kinder toward self and others. We're all in this pain-soaked life-and-death journey together. Kindness enables us to exemplify our bedrock kinship. There is never a wrong time or way to be kind. "What does the Eternal require of you, but to do justice, and to love kindness, and to walk humbly with your God?"

What does humility have to do with being an ever-evolving lover? Everything! We need humility, because arrogance builds barriers, not crossings, between individuals, clans, countries, and species. We need humility, since brash egos hanker for personal credit rather than shared acknowledgment. We need humility, because, although human beings are marvelous works of art, we are neither the Infinite One nor the center piece of creation. As St. Bernard of Clairvaux (1090-1153) couched it: "There are four cardinal virtues—humility, humility, humility, and humility."

We are charged to walk humbly with ourselves, with our neighbors, and with all living entities. Additionally, we are called neither to walk in front of God in haughtiness nor behind in servility, but alongside as bona fide partners in stewarding "the interdependent web of all existence." And notice that Micah directs us to walk humbly with *our* personal understanding of God, not the conviction of somebody else.

But walking humbly doesn't allow us to wander off into apathy or laziness at this juncture in our lives. Just because we can't do everything, it doesn't mean we can't do the things that you and I are uniquely gifted and charged to contribute.

And, as noted earlier, if we can't *walk*, you and I know what to do: keep on moving humbly . . . with *humor* and *humaneness* all the way to the *humus*—our final resting ground.

XV. *Am I up-to-date with forgiving and being forgiven?*

It's not that I'm oblivious to the underbelly or weediness,
but I've had to forgive myself for so many things,
that it's very hard to hold too much against other people.
—Kay Montgomery

As I noted in the introduction, nowhere in our UU Principles and Sources, our foundational document, is *forgiveness* to be found, a virtue that Protestant theologian Reinhold Niebuhr rightfully calls "the final form of love"—and stated openly (#461) in our own hymnal.

We humans are prone to bypass forgiveness, racing with lightning speed from our hurts to conciliation without recognizing what must be forgiven before any durable healing can take hold. Truces are often made and signed, then broken before the ink is dry. That's happened all too frequently in the Middle East and Ireland. America's been party to its share of busted treaties as well, starting and continuing with our indigenous peoples.

Furthermore, there has to be sufficient pause between the offense and any reconciliation, so that genuine forgiveness can evolve. How tempting it is to rush toward redemption, especially when our heart isn't on the block, engaging in what has been called "forgiveness lite." I recall, early in my ministry, inviting a grief-stricken person to begin the process of forgiveness toward someone who had murdered his wife. And he plaintively cried: "Oh, Pastor Tom, not yet, not yet, not yet!"

I was moving toward a premature pardon, out of some purportedly "noble" theology combined with my own raw uneasiness, rather than caring about this person's fresh loss and indescribable suffering. To do the opposite: to confront our hurts, to pursue responsible restitution, to allow people to grieve properly . . . are crucial steps in the course toward genuine reconciliation.

Forgiveness has nothing to do with excusing, explaining, or forgetting but everything to do with remembering. Plus, real forgiveness is always concerned with full answerability. Mahatma Gandhi's forgiveness was accompanied by his bold and relentless actions to end British imperialism in India. Dr. Martin Luther King, Jr. forgave lynch mobs, even as he worked for laws to protect all citizens from such mobs.

When it's genuine, forgiveness must remain an option not an obsession. While not overlooking ugliness and fracture, forgiveness charges us to surrender antipathy and to forfeit pride. Forgiveness may be excruciatingly demanding and costly (it may even prove unworkable in certain situations); however, the evidence shows that non-forgivers—chiefly as we age and approach the end of life—often pay a severe emotional price in refusing to risk restoration.

Bitterness is the culprit that sabotages forgiveness. It is a diminishing emotion, digging two graves, yours and that of your target. The word resentment is derived from the Latin meaning "to feel again." The non-forgiver, then, can become someone who often feels and reacts to the pain again and again, caught in the round of spite. It's no surprise that in the recovery movement, resentment is known as "the number one offender."

In the long run, most human beings desire to break these vicious cycles of hatred and revenge. We want to bury the hatchet, move beyond animosity and toward some semblance of forgiveness, even if it's partial. Dropping grudges and clearing bitterness are probably our greatest desire and need as we face dying squarely. We crave to accomplish what Rev. Rob Eller-Isaacs references in his "Litany of Atonement" (#637): "We forgive ourselves and each other; we begin again in love."

When we're able to do so, here are some suggestions.

First, forgiveness is not a single act so much as a constant attitude. Jesus told the scribes: "seventy-times-seven" (Matthew 18:22) which, of course, spurs us to quit keeping score and stick to forgiving . . . morning, noon, and night.

Second, whenever we need and want to forgive, we should go ahead and do so. It isn't necessary to tell the person we are forgiving that they are the subject of our efforts. The same rule obtains after forgiveness occurs. We have no obligation to tell the people we have forgiven that we have done so. Sometimes it helps; often it doesn't. Forgiveness doesn't have to be reciprocal in order to prove salutary.

Third, we can forgive the dead as well as the living. People die, but bonds survive. Every relationship that lodges in our heart can be meaningfully engaged and healed.

Fourth, forgiveness is just as hard to receive as to give. Forgiveness is difficult to give, because we need to see the one who hurt us as other than the hurt, and that isn't easy or comfortable. Forgiveness is difficult to receive, because we need to believe that someone has seen more in us than the hurtful thing we did.

Fifth, it is never too late or impossible to forgive. If it takes us to forgive or be forgiven, on our death bed, so be it. Hallelujah!

Sixth, there is no one way to forgive. It all depends on the situation and the people involved. But the same motivation universally applies: setting imprisoned people free, both forgiver and forgiven.

Finally, who needs to be forgiven? The list is endless, and all our names are on it. We need to forgive individuals and institutions as well as countries—our own, plus foreign ones. God could use our forgiveness too. Most critically, we need to forgive ourselves. We will never be able to receive another's forgiveness, unless we do so.

Forgiveness is both a sublime and grueling enterprise. It comprises the power that saves us from spiritual decay, the hope that overcomes haunting despair, and the love that frees us to complete our dying days.

XVI. *How am I creating beauty in my closing days on Earth?*

With all its crushing sorrow and aching loss, life is still strung beads of miraculous beauty. Beauty is the order we bring out of chaos. Beauty is also the way we treat one another in our interactions: our kindness, our care, our tenderness. Wouldn't a world without beauty be unbearable?
—Carolyn Sheets Owen-Towle

As Ecclesiastes 3:11 puts it: "God has made everything beautiful in its own time." The Eternal One has spawned beauty in multifarious figures and essences of animals, plants, elements, and humans. A baby is beautiful in a way distinct from a young adult from a dying senior.

Our life-long job is never to lose sight of our peculiar and enduring magnificence. And we remain beautiful not as in pretty, unruffled, or glamorous but beautiful as in never ceasing to be rare and wondrous creations.

During our elder years, it's the optimal time to experience moments and expressions of genuine beauty beneath the glitziness and superficiality with which our lives are bombarded. I don't simply mean producing quilts or crafting poetry, although there's ample spark and time to do that during COVID-19. I'm essentially referring to home-stretchers soaking in the full-blown beauty of existence. The Navajos of North America put it vividly in our hymnal (#682):

Beauty is before me, and
Beauty is behind me,
above me and below me
hovers the beautiful.
I am surrounded by it,
I am immersed in it.

In my youth, I am aware of it,
and, in old age,
I shall walk quietly
the beautiful trail.
In beauty, it is begun.
In beauty, it is ended.

Here's an anecdote of a professed "Gray Panther" in one of my early congregations. On her birthday, Millie was receiving congratulations. And a grandchild said to her, "Grandma, you're beautiful!" Without a moment's hesitation, Millie replied, "Well, I ought to be. I'm 84; so my beauty isn't decorative anymore; it's structural!" That's the attitude we elders and crones need to inspirit as we mosey deathward.

There has been no mightier tussle in our progressive movement during the past century plus than reclaiming the missing link in Ralph Waldo Emerson's trilogy of "truth, goodness, and beauty." Beauty, for all intents and purposes, has been considered our weak or lost cousin, veritably absent from our theological landscape.

However, over the decades of our consolidated existence since 1961, the verdict has become manifest: Unitarian Universalism, to become a full-service faith, will need to balance its analytical mind with an appreciative one. Maximum employment of both our left and right brains is required to fan our flaming chalice. And we seniors can lead the way by bearing and creating beauty all the way to our graves.

While I was serving on our Commission on Appraisal (2003-2009), it became clear that beauty was widely affirmed as a premier yet unacknowledged source in our theology, reflected in the monumental drive, from adherents across the continent, promoting revisions for Article II. The Reverend Richard Davis crystallized it this way:

> There is a seventh source that has not been recognized and affirmed. That source is art.
>
> This is how I would describe it: "the living tradition that we share draws from many sources including the Creative Arts: which reveal to us the face of life's beauty and joy, its enduring truth and meaning and which opens our hearts to feelings of awe and gratitude.
>
> Art and spirituality are so intertwined that they cannot be separated.

Sadly, all of the amendments incorporating spiritual themes such as beauty, evil, death, God, and forgiveness were thwarted due to procedural blockages at our General Assembly in 2009. But the beat goes on, and, someday, this geezer hopes and prays that *beauty* will be given its rightful place among our primary theological sources.

One of the touchstones that fortify my aging spirit is the lovely poem written by the Irish bard, William Butler Yeats (1865-1939): "Sailing to Byzantium." Composed in his early sixties, it constitutes Yeats' ode to the creative expansiveness required to keep humans vital when our souls are "fastened to a dying animal"—a fragile, failing corpus. Yeats bespeaks the triumph of beauty over death. Here's but a patch:

An aged one is but a paltry thing,
a tattered coat upon a stick, unless
soul clap its hands and sing, and louder sing
for every tatter in its mortal dress.

Truly, our life-long mission is to recognize, then internalize, our vocation as creators not destroyers. As our lives edge closer toward completion, we can leave behind gifts of splendor and loveliness. It matters not whether our creative response is a painting, a garden, a dance, an afghan, or some caring, wonder-filled deed. The goal is having our "soul clap its hands and sing . . . "

Beauty can be found and formed in the midst of travail and injustice. Thoreau spoke of "severe beauty," by which I assume he meant that a moment or exchange may often be abrasive and harsh, but still beautiful. The manifold expressions of beauty displayed during our pandemic furnish abundant evidence of that truth.

The word "fair" refers to something lovely but also to something just; for fairness yokes the worlds of beauty and justice. As colleague Edward Harris professes: "Fair people keep their commitments, give fair gifts, and forgive fairly. Try love as fairness. Life isn't fair, but love can be." So can beauty.

Beholding or generating beauty lights our inner fire. Beauty can arouse the capacity, in human beings, to become bolder, better selves. Deeper beauty is known to occasion sounder truth and broader goodness in our religious lives, personally and communally. Our homestretch mission is to embody Plotinus's sage phrase: "those who behold beauty become themselves beautiful."

There exists no finer way to close out life than with the words of Emily Elizabeth Dickinson (1830-1886):

Beauty crowds me till I die
Beauty, mercy have on me
But if I expire today
Let it be in sight of thee

Amen.

XVII. *If I were to die shortly, what might I wish to say or do in my*
      closing days?

Today is a good day to die, "hoka hey" (all is accomplished).
—Lakota tribe

Thanatologist and spiritual teacher Stephen Levine (1937-2016) frames this query in a slightly different way: "If you were going to die soon and had only one phone call you could make, who would you call and what would you say? And why are you waiting?" I've got two or three folks that come right to mind. I'm confident you do as well.

Here's another way to pose this question: if given the opportunity, what might your final words be to a nurse, the kind one, as well as the surly one; to someone long dead, still purring in your soul; to an unreconciled friend or family member; to an animal not your own; to a political opponent or religious foe; and to an unborn child in a foreign land? These are demanding questions to answer, but that's why we're focusing on *Mindful Dying*, because the enterprise prompts us to make sufficient (not perfect) peace as we saunter toward our expiration. All I'm requiring of readers and participants is for us to stay ever "mindful!"

If I were given but ten minutes to live, here's what I envision doing. I would share three minutes with loved ones who are able or wish to visit me; one meditating upon some passage from religious literature; one minute weeping over a still frozen or fractured personal or global situation; another one belly-laughing; two in quiet confession and gratitude; and two minutes singing.

But, then again, as death draws nigh, I might change my mind. How about you? Let's swap notes.

XVIII. *What are some elements that would constitute a good or fitting death for me?*

Come down, death, right easy.
—Old song which Virginia slaves would sing at their funerals

- A good death permits me to be pretty much the same person dying as I was when alive . . . maybe even a tad better.
- A good death doesn't mean I'll die peacefully, although I'd like that.
- A good death is more than going to sleep one night and not waking up, although I'll take that too.
- A good death is going-well, well-going, going-well, well-going . . . and all of what that phrase might mean. The Buddhist term is *sugato* meaning "excellent realization."
- A good death is extinction with significance.
- A good death doesn't contradict the conduct of my vocation, partnership, family, citizenship, religion, and way of life.
- A good death is when she/he/they may experience the Latin farewell: *requiescat in pace.*
- A good death is when we go into the ground essentially scrubbed of regrets and resentments—flush with rejoicing.

But, clearly, there are more questions that need to be addressed such as logistical ones about where and how and when? Let's start with location. Almost 90% of my parishioners have yearned to die at home or in an abode of familiar surroundings and company. But that can't always happen, can it?

My beloved Mom needed to enter a nursing home the final months of her life and she told us, after days in her room shared with two other farewell voyagers: "Dear ones, my world is small but good." My brother and I would visit as often as we could, other family and friends did as well, and her church comrades were loyal and caring.

It wasn't Mom's first choice, but she died, sufficiently at peace, in this nursing facility with a bedside table upon which stood photographs of her husband, Harold, her two sons, Phil and Tom, and the Bible flush to her favorite passage: "I have learned in whatsoever state I am in, therewith, to be content . . . " (Philippians 4:11)

Taped to the wall was a butcher sheet posting the assertion of one of her grand-daughters: "Grandma, do you know how much you are loved!" Note Erin employed an exclamation point rather than a question mark!

The next query is more nuanced: Do you wish to die alone or accompanied? Or would you, perchance, choose a mixture of both?

Solitude is a multilayered condition. We are born via a relationship, but we emerge from the womb, stark-naked, yelping as we burst from sheltered privacy into an exposed, noisy scene. We also exit alone, and even the interlude between birth and death—whether painful, loving, boring, happy, or a blend of all—finds us primarily alone. "Alone, alone, all, all alone, alone on a wide, wide sea" penned the poet Coleridge.

It's my personal and professional experience that golden agers wrangle most intensely with the dragon of aloneness. As our family and friends move away or die off, we're increasingly lonesome. Yet, as Colombian author Gabriel Garcia Marquez (1927-2014) sagely notes: "The secret of a good old age is simply making an honorable pact with solitude." Truly, a healthy homestretch, right up until dissolution, requires "making an honorable pact" with our original condition: aloneness on this earth.

And I burst into singing another spiritual:
Jesus walked this lonesome valley. He had to walk it by himself.
Oh, nobody else could walk it for him. He had to walk it by himself.

The rabbi isn't alone in walking life's lonesome valley. The hymn invites the rest of us to join the arduous trek: "we must walk this lonesome valley by ourselves;" then, "we must go and stand our trial by ourselves" as well.

Of course, as long as another human is nearby, we can connect, and we do. Elders exude feelings, exchange ideas, and intertwine bodies, even while we're dying. Countless home-stretchers connect with mounting intensity, from marrow to marrow. Here's a touching example of enduring love demonstrated by a couple in our congregation.

Wilma was dying of rectal cancer. Her husband, Eduardo, sat at Wilma's bedside, holding his beloved's hands, talking to and crying with her. A nurse came into the room. "Excuse me, sir," she said, gently tapping Eduardo's shoulder. "It's time to change the bandages. If you'd please leave the room, I'll be done in just a few minutes." "Excuse me," Eduardo replied with a mellow but determined smile, "but I'll stay right here. This *tush* and I have had a lot of good times together. I'm not going to turn my back on it now!"

Such tender displays of affection aren't always the way we die. Often our family can't be present, or our friends do turn their backs on us. In any case, when all is said and done, there's a profound sense in which we live alone and die alone. There exist places in each of us that can never be visited, even by loved ones. In our deepest moments of communion, we live, at best, *beside,* rather than *inside,* another.

But there's more complexity. For some of us, after we've shared moments of human connection and intimacy, we truly desire to exit alone. A quiet room and a still heart deliver the peacefulness we seek. I personally want to spend my final ticks with the source of "everlasting love."

So, I guess I'm asking us to consider riding one final paradox: to die alone . . . together. Put theologically, if our existential condition is aloneness; our essential call is community. And we carry out our destiny in the interplay between the two. Living-and-dying includes both.

XIX. *How do I wish to die spiritually?*

Few of us will die exactly as we plan or hope. There are too many unknown factors. Plus, we're rarely in control of our dying. Hence, we must remain trustful agnostics.

I fondly recall the superlative Swedish diplomat, economist, author, second Secretariat-General of the United Nations, Dag Hammarskjöld (1905-1961) who was tragically killed in a plane crash *en route* to cease-fire negotiations. Stolen away too early. Whether you or I get 2 or 10 or 30 or 60 more years, Dag's pledge insists: "If only I may grow firmer, simpler, quieter, warmer." I certainly don't want to die tragically like Hammarskjöld did, but I hanker to embody the spiritual virtues of his exemplary pledge.

The following list is not the "best" or "right" one; it's simply mine, and yours will be yours. And mine will likely be revised, when I draw closer to my final breath. But for now, four interlinking, spiritual qualities rise to the top: serenity, gratitude, gentleness, and merrymaking.

UU colleague Jane Rzepka reflects upon serenity:

The statue on my bureau is about four feet long and maybe a foot tall. A reclining Buddha. I bought it because he lies there radiating serenity in spite of his situation, whatever it is. Sleeping, resting, enlightened or dead. Buddha's okay with being on death's door, and I like seeing that when I wake up in the morning.

Whenever I sit and imagine my own dying, my mind is besieged with emotions and thoughts, and more thoughts . . . until I quiet down, close my eyes, doze off and enter the silence. As *homo sapiens*, we are bidden to reach accord with what's achievable and with what remains during what psychoanalyst Carl Jung rightly named "our winter of grace."

Serenity means dissolving into the ultimate stillness, "clinging to naught."

My mother was the poster person for serenity, remaining essentially content throughout the entirety of her 95+ years on this planet. Mom wasn't always untroubled and cloudless, since she bit her nails just as I pick my nose. Perhaps you have an irksome habit as well. Nonetheless, Mother Mary routinely exemplified the virtue that the Shona tribe in Zimbabwe calls *rufaro*: an abiding sense of equanimity. Neither highs nor lows appeared to rattle Mom's cage.

Mom wasn't a fatalist, because she passionately labored for constructive changes in her world. She wasn't passive or acquiescent. Resonating with Dr. Martin Luther King, Jr.'s phrase "creative maladjustment" kept our mother ethically responsive and spiritually sane. She was a relentless campaigner for racial equality and the only person on her Presbyterian Church session that stood tall for gay liberation and rights. Mom was a quiet yet persevering radical. She would have received one of the "shameless agitator" awards that our First UU Church in San Diego has handed out annually.

Most of the time, Mom gave up wanting what she didn't already have and learned how to bear what she could not change. She accepted the workings of the ecosphere; then she aligned herself with them. Mary Catherine Flanagan Towle straddled being content but never satisfied.

Mom's sense of repose was shown in her willingness to die when her time came. She was neither fascinated with nor fixated on her death; she rarely talked about it. Yet as death drew nigh, Mother Mary faced it not with rage, resentment, or regret but with abundant *rufaro*.

Every time I sing the Beatles' last major hit, *Let It Be*, released in 1970, shortly after their break-up as a group, I think of my mother, as well as my cherished mother-in-law, Mary Baskerville Sheets, who exhibited a similar temperament:

When I find myself in times of trouble,
Mother Mary comes to me,
    speaking words of wisdom,
let it be . . .

In her dying days, our mother transmitted no new enlightenment; in fact, there were, finally, no words at all. Mutual and abiding love resided in the gentle clutch of our hands and the waterfall of our moist eyes. Somewhat restless of body, Mary's spirit seemed pacific, and her face emitted the same affection that it had shown the world since her arrival.

As our brain, heart, and limbs irreversibly age, may a sense of contentedness prevail. May we dwell in a state of what the Buddhists fittingly call: "calm abiding." May we garner sufficient peace—free at last from futile churning. May we harmonize with what is, with what is, with what is . . .

I consider that to be the essential meaning of progressive theologian Reinhold Niebuhr's (1951) serenity prayer. If there was ever a time to internalize this entreaty, it's during our consummation.

God, grant me the serenity to accept the things I cannot change,
the courage to change the things I can,
and the wisdom to know the difference.

Then, I hope to depart basking in gratitude. I concur with the sentiment of author Annie Dillard: "Say thank you rather than please when facing death." There's a time and place to beg and barter during the tattered course of our lives. It's a natural part of our human make-up to fancy and covet something else, but death is the occasion, is it not, to burst forth in sheer thankfulness for a life unexpected and unearned?

Religions have always spoken about *redeeming* time. Nearing the ripened age of 80-years-old, I finally fathom what that theological concept might mean. We tend to be concerned with loading up our time, but religion says: "Wait a minute! That's not it. The point of life is to redeem time. Lots of people save time; your true mission is to relish time." We fill time through driven activity, by staying mindlessly occupied or by being extremely efficient. But we fulfill time by making the most of our moments—giving back excellence, love, and joy to the Spirit that escorted us into being.

Time is a gift. Each day of our journey is unearned. None of our moments is guaranteed. Hence, we're beckoned to be thankful for every extension we receive upon waking in the morning. I can't think of a finer daily prayer than something humble yet heartfelt: "Thank you God, thank you Cosmos . . . just plain thanks for yet another day of living and loving, come what may."

Most every morning, I engage in a Nepalese body prayer introduced to me by ministerial sister, Orlanda Brugnola. My homespun version of this ancient ritual unfurls the day, keeping me on soulful track. This prayer stretches every limb of the Self. I invite readers to render your own amendments to my routine, for that's the way of useful and ripened spiritual practice.

Upon rising from bed, I plant my feet firmly on the floor, typically following a jaunt to the bathroom. After finding my body's center of gravity, I slightly bend my knees and cup my hands in a receptive mode, right above the navel. I affirm my core with words such as: "I am a child of the universe. I belong here. It's good for me to be alive."

Then I raise my hands, barely touching, fully stretched to the sky in a prayerful gesture, and I continue speaking out loud: "i thank You God for most this amazing day" (Unitarian e. e. cummings) or comparable words of bone-deep gratitude.

When my arms reach their apex, I open wide my hands, shape them into a chalice to contain all the manifold comforts and burdens to be delivered on this day. My words stream: "Into my hands are welcomed today's delights and difficulties, sorrows and joys." Then slowly, in circling fashion, I draw my extended hands back to the beginning position, while asserting: "I promise to spread these blessings among all living entities I greet on this priceless day."

I repeat this ritual of gratitude, perhaps three or four times, to stretch my being in bounteous measure. After performing this body-and-soul exercise, the day consistently tastes better. It keeps my body energetic and my spirit limber . . . moving on the pathway toward the pinnacle of my life.

Our colleague, Nancy Shaffer, had a large tumor removed from her brain in 2011. During the course of her closing months of life, Shaffer crafted an inspirational book, *While Still There is Light*, focusing upon gratitude:

The only question large enough is how to give enough thanks for our lives. That's the beginning: large enough thanks.

I harmonize with Rev. Nancy's quest. Breathing with a soul chockfull of thankfulness is how I wish to expire.

I'm always elevated by the enchanting story told by Unitarian Universalist G. Peter Fleck (1909-1995), who was a successful international banker and venture capitalist:

I am not afraid to die, but sometimes I am afraid about how I'll get there from here. For on the way, many suffer illness, anxiety and pain, loneliness and the loss of independence, until Death comes to them as a friend and takes them into its everlasting arms. Besides, I sometimes feel that dying, that is leaving this world, is not my responsibility but that of the Power that brought me into this world. And I trust that Power.

Our oldest daughter, age five, gave this answer to her four-year-old sister who had anxiously inquired about dying: "It's nothing to be afraid of. It's just as if you were invited somewhere, and it's getting late and you go to the hostess and you say: 'Thank you for the wonderful party. I really enjoyed myself, but now it is time to go home.'"

Our final home can never be adequately described, but my heartfelt hunch is that it will be restful and abounding in love. No other data about our ultimate destiny is either furnished or needed.

Bart Giamatti (1938-1989), Professor of English Renaissance Literature and the seventh commissioner of Major League baseball, died after serving only five months in office. He couldn't have depicted more eloquently the linkage between baseball and life's homestretch:

Baseball is about homecoming. It is a journey by theft and strength, guile and speed, out around first to the far island of second, where foes lurk in the reefs and the green sea suddenly grows deeper, then to turn sharply, skimming the shallows, making for a shore that will show a friendly face, a color, a familiar language, and, at third, to proceed, no longer by paths indirect but straight, to home.

So, here I am, a full-blown elder, rounding third base and dashing (make that, clambering) straightway toward home plate. Since we're still amidst the pandemic, there are no cheering or jeering fans in the stands.

Plus, I'm no longer occupied with scoring the winning run; simply reaching home base—the place of my origin, "everlasting love"—will suffice.

Another quality of a "good death" is going gently. I choose to quibble with Dylan Thomas (1914-1953), Welsh poet whose most famous piece was:

Do not go gentle into that good night,
old age should burn and rave at close of day;
rage, rage against the dying of the light.

During my homestretch years, there might well come a time to "burn and rave" as my windows squeak and doors shut. Nonetheless, my topmost desire remains to close out life quietly and tenderly—traveling ever-so gently into the next stage. Dying skyward or dying earthward, entering the light or entering the darkness—either route suits me fine. My only aspiration is peacefully returning to the loving Source of All.

For me, an equivalence of gentleness is softness. The Zen master Dogen, back in 1227, returning to Japan after spending many years in China with great Zen masters, was asked what he had learned about the process of living-and-dying. And he calmingly offered: "Softness of heart, softness of heart."

Miles Beauchamp, a journalist member of one of my interim congregations, frames it movingly:

Water is soft, fluid, and extremely strong.
It will carve away rock. Strong, patient, and never ceasing.
Be soft, flowing, and surrounding life.

On the road back home toward death, our spines need to be straight as a rail, our bellies firm not flabby, and our minds frank and staunch, but our hearts are summoned to be gentle and soft without being sappy. A sound farewell mantra is called DROPS: "Don't resist or push, soften!" Be like water.

Finally, I desire some merrymaking. As already referenced in *Making Peace with Our Death*, I hope to sing my heart out as I die. Being a merrymaker graces the re-firement card in my wallet, and crooning is implanted in my DNA. George Bernard Shaw (1856-1950), Irish playwright and political activist, exclaimed: "I want to be thoroughly used up when I die . . . " My token amendment: I want to be thoroughly "sung out" when I die.

A celebrated organist, perhaps it was Bach, reported that music training as a child was no more and no less than "practicing the scales of rejoicing." Well, singing's been my foremost mode of "practicing the scales of rejoicing." Before death consumes me, and as my voice is willing, I want to sing some sort of thank you to God and all living entities for a blessed journey beyond my imagining. I hardly know what tunes I'll choose to sing, since there's so much music crowding my soul.

However, one of the ballads will definitely be *Amazing Grace* (#205 or #206):

Amazing grace! How sweet the sound, that saved a wretch (soul) like me!
I once was lost, but now am found,
Was blind but now I see.

'Twas grace that taught my heart to fear,
and grace my fears relieved;
how precious did that grace appear the hour I first believed!

Through many dangers, toils, and snares,
I have already come; 'tis grace that brought me safe thus far,
and grace will lead me home.

When we've been here ten thousand years, bright shining as the
sun,
We've no less days to sing God's praise
than when we'd first begun.

And here are two additional verses, composed by Unitarian Universalist songster, Nell Lutz—words that dispense solace as well:

'Tis love that taught me not to fear;
'Tis love that set me free.
For love is life and life is love;
I'll go where love leads me.

When I have lived my lifetime here
and loved all humankind;
I'll have what I can never lose,
for human love's divine.

I'm not sure there's a more fitting deathbed canticle for a Universalist Unitarian such as I am. Furthermore, I sing this hymn consistently at all three of my nursing homes; hence, I'm in solid spiritual and vocal shape to warble it homeward bound. Currently, that is.

When all is said and done, after slogging through swamps of terror and ecstasy, periods of being ungraceful and ungracious, we humanoids are still damn lucky, statistical miracles, and privileged to have experienced any seasons of splendor and emptiness. All is grace. Amazing grace.

In addition to considering the "spiritual" state in which we wish to die, I would recommend another end-of-life ritual. I modify Stephen Levine's "Guided Meditation on Our Own Dying." We turn toward and take dying in. Our thoughts play with the idea that our body is dying, then is gone. This contemplative exercise can be usefully processed in a group setting (we've shared it in *Mindful Dying* workshops) or in consort with a loved one.

XX.   *What do I plan to do with my body or physical remains?*

When I die, it will be an honor for my blood to return to the sea and my bones to become the sand. Reassured, I am called back to my life, to another day.
—Elizabeth Tarbox

I invite readers to shift gears now to make plans for choices following your physical cessation. How do you wish to dispose of your corpus? Again, no right answer, only your decision. But unless you're deliberating before you die, your relatives will be confused or even engage in needless squabbles, when forced to make "your" judgment for you. As a pastor, I can attest to such disputes.

First off, Carolyn and I belong to a memorial society in our local community, so we've already registered our wishes for disposition there, as well as placing them in the church office records, and finally in our ubiquitous *Green Book*. If you haven't already made such worthwhile arrangements, go forth and do so. Again, make sure you convey to your family and loved ones the specifics and whereabouts of your end-of-life material.

Some of us want to be buried in cemeteries where other family members reside. Others will be gifting our bodily remains to medical science (so get that matter squared away with your chosen hospital). Many moderns are turning to the *Green Burial* option wherein the interment of the body is placed in the soil in a manner that does not inhibit decomposition but allows the dead person to be naturally recycled. It is an alternative to the contemporary Western burial and cremation methods and funerary customs.

There's a sad, rather grotesque, fact about the legendary Lebanese poet, Kahlil Gibran (1883-1931), who was buried in a setting similar to that of a second-rate saint. Romantics, like I am, loathe this story, but we've got to face the multifaceted truths about our heroes and heroines. Gibran is buried in a gift shop. He lies in state, the coffin covered with plastic flowers, counters on either side hawking souvenirs, in an old monastery at Bsherri in the highlands of Lebanon. Gibran abhorred the cheap and the superficial, the ugly and the fake, so it's ironic that such was his fate. Only intellectual snobs would gloat, saying that a sentimental, popular poet deserves a grave in a souvenir store. I personally find Gibran's poetry and prose on death, partnership, and children profound not shallow. They have always furnished foundational readings for my rites-of-passage as a pastor. In planning your own last rites, where might you choose to be buried?

Returning to the ground makes both physical and spiritual sense. After all, our entire earthly journey is primarily about finding solid ground, common ground, battleground, safe ground, tilling ground, and sacred ground . . . then returning to the ground of our being. I beam with the fancy of German biologist/philosopher, Andreas Weber (1967-): "I've consumed in life, but in death, I'll be consumed. I think they'll find me delicious."

How about cremation? Let's get technically descriptive for a moment. Cremation is the combustion, vaporization, and oxidation of cadavers to basic chemical compounds, such as gases, ashes, and mineral fragments retaining the appearance of dry bone. Our oldest child has made it clear that he doesn't want this method, being nervous around fires, dead or alive. So, his heartfelt wishes will be honored with a casket. Three cheers for our clan: we're talking specifics about death with our offspring. More needs to be shared, but we're on our way. How's your tribe progressing with conversations about dying and death?

I personally prefer cremation but have not formalized the precise location yet. After the gracious and generous grinding, my ashes might be placed in an old cardboard shoe box, formerly cradling prized baseball cards, or in an exquisite festooned urn or poured in the ground next to my beloved's or scattered to the four winds in a favorite forest or waterway. Most likely, they will be dispersed in the canyon behind our First Church sanctuary where Carolyn and I have scattered countless other cremains, including those of our parents. How about you, my friend?

XXI. *What happens after I die? Or what constitutes my theology of post-death?*

When the tenth-century Chinese Zen master Dasui Fazhen was asked, "How are you doing at the time when life-death arrives?" he answered promptly, "When served tea, I take tea; when served a meal, I take a meal." In sum, whatever happens after you die, you merely take it in. It may not be what you expected, or it may match your final wish. Be a good trooper. Of course, what else can you do?

There will always remain a range of viewpoints as to what happens to us when we die. After all, each of us is free to draw our own hunches concerning post-death. Remember the Christian passage: "Wisdom is justified by all her children . . . " (Luke 7:35), and the word for "salvation" in the Hebrew Scriptures connotes a broad and spacious place.

Carolyn and I recall, when preaching on death, that we once unflinchingly asked how many worshippers believed in immortality of influence, resurrection of the body, nothingness, continuing consciousness, reincarnation, or some other position. Clusters of hands were raised throughout the congregation for every conceivable opinion. And likely, some hands weren't even raised. Diversity reigns supreme in our religious fold. So, I invite, nay urge, each reader to internalize your given perspective on post-death reality, and then continue to update it, all the way to your grave.

Hopefully, the subsequent examples of post-death thought will ignite your own reflections. Once more, they are not in any order of priority.

(1) When life is over, life is over. When you're dead, you're dead. You are stuck in a state of nothingness. Dust unto dust.

(2) American journalist Katy Butler says: "My deeds are my only companions. They are the ground upon which I stand." Or as Albert Schweitzer avowed: "My life—my argument."

In short, let my life speak for itself.

(3) Unknown

His friend and fellow abolitionist Parker Pillsbury called upon Henry David Thoreau wanting to talk about the afterlife, a topic of substantial interest to Pillsbury, especially being a former minister. Hoping to coax out some clearer vision of the world to come, Pillsbury pressed: "You seem so near the brink of the dark river that I almost wonder how the opposite shore may appear to you, Henry?"

The wily Thoreau quipped, "One world at a time! One world at a time!" Thoreau gave his fullest self to the present moment, this natural world, the only one he knew and the home he cared about—"the real, solid, sincere" terrain of corporeal existence. He left matters concerning the next realm totally up to the Creator.

(4) "Death into new life."

Parker Palmer, a premier Quaker thinker and one-time associate of mine from Beloit College back in the 1960's, frames it this way:

I won't be shocked if death has surprises in store for me. Amid my unknowing, I am sure of two things: when we die, our bodies return to the earth, and earth knows how to turn death into new life.

I find Palmer's perspective satisfying, even reassuring.

(5) Returning to "Everlasting Love"

While in sympathy with various aspects of the aforementioned convictions, my dominant view is essentially Universalist, a theological standpoint that concurs with the Song of Solomon that "love is stronger than death"—yes, love outlasts and triumphs over death. Upon death, we enter the embrace of "everlasting love."

No one describes this theological outlook more strikingly than one of my ministerial mentors, Gordon "Bucky" McKeeman (1920-2013):

Universalism is not faith in the inevitability of heaven which supports me as I face death but faith in the reality of love. The old Universalist heresy claimed that God's love knew no limits and would find the sinner no matter how far from holiness she or he strayed. The fundamental nature of reality is love.

(6) Resurrection of the Body

First, it must be noted that the resurrection experience of the risen Jesus in the early church, whatever its source and however interpreted, did not itself generate the belief in the resurrection of the dead. Such a belief was already an accepted view of the time.

When you study primitive religions, you find that survival after death is one of the earliest mystical hypotheses, related probably to some deep biological craving of our human organism. Christianity responded to that passion as well as to the pressing need to establish an organized religion by proclaiming as doctrine, miracles such as the bodily resurrection of Jesus.

Furthermore, the Apostle Paul, whose letters to fledgling

churches are the oldest Christian writings, says literally nothing about the details of the resurrection. It's a truism that we have no accounts of the resurrection *per se*, but only of the events which followed the resurrection.

Still this is standard Christian doctrine, and there are surely Unitarian Universalists who believe it as well.

(7) Eternal or heavenly bliss

Let me launch with the jest of English writer and lay theologian, G. K. Chesterton (1874-1936): "There are people who pray for eternal life and don't know what to do with themselves on a rainy Sunday." I would add, let alone during an extended home-stay due to COVID-19.

I admit to finding most notions of eternal life or paradise uninteresting. It would be nice in many cases, although not all, to reconnect with departed friends or loved ones, but not to endure an interminable sameness of our bonds. Without the presence of exertion, even trouble, perpetual heaven would prove oppressively bland. Did you ever hear an evangelist de-scribe heaven in terms of the challenges waiting to be faced or in terms of passion or toil or justice? No, it's always an Elysian Fields, characterized by terrible constancy, with no further growth or change taking place, destitute of variation or wres-tling. How eternally boring!

But I confess to singing lustily "Swing Low, Sweet Chariot," "Oh, When the Saints Go Marching In," and other heaven-based ballads in every nursing home I frequent, so I'm hardly a purist.

(8) Reincarnation

Reincarnation is the rebirth of the soul in a new body. So, the key question remains: do you want a continuation of your old body, spruced up some, or do you hanker for a totally virginal corpus? And in what century, family, country, racialized and gender identity might you choose to reappear?

When the Zen guide was asked what his future life might be like, he candidly said: "Let me be a donkey or a horse and work for the villagers!" I resonate with this master. If my presence extends in any new form, I want to be employed, usefully, as a practical servant or as an animal that labors.

(9) Immortality of Influence

Death leaves a heartache no one can heal.
Love leaves a memory no one can steal.
—Headstone in Ireland

As Unitarian Universalist sympathizer, Norman Cousins (1915-1990), put it: "Our passport to immortality, to be valid, must have the stamp of the human community upon it." In short, our lives will be measured by whether our contributions have transcended ego gratification and served the universal good, in one way or another. This is called the "rippling effect" wherein each of us creates, often without plan or awareness, rings of inspiration that may impact others for years, even generations, after our death.

Lest we get carried away with self-importance, at some point, memories of our singular character will become jumbled, even fade. Descendants will turn to more pressing matters, and those who knew us personally will die. Eventually, our distinctiveness and accomplishments will shrivel, likely vanish.

Emily Levine, philosophical comedian, dying of cancer, minces no words: "You're going to be forgotten at some point, so get over it!"

Carolyn's father, Millard Owen Sheets, was a famous and productive artist, and, 31+ years after his death, continues to be remembered daily in Internet posts and website references, as well as folks viewing his paintings in museums and homes and appreciating his sculptured buildings scattered far and wide. But few mortals enjoy such longevity of influence.

Some Unitarian Universalists posit a mystical sense of immortality. The idiosyncratic energy we incarnated during our earthly sojourn flows back to the center of Creation. Planetary life is amended because we existed. Undeniably, this is good news.

Another variation is living on primarily through the forces of the natural world. We perish physically and our bodies disperse to the winds and tumble earthward, but our souls survive in myriad ways and sites, known and unknown, foreign and familiar. Birago Diop, Senegalese poet and storyteller, confirms this approach:

> *Those who are dead are never gone: they are in the tree that*
> *rustles,*
> *the wood that groans, in the water that sleeps, in the breast*
> *of the woman,*
> *in the child who is wailing, the grasses that weep,*
> *in the whispering rocks, in the forest.*

(10) Nirvana

When the heart is without anxiety or obstruction then there is no fear. When confusion and illusion are distant, that is true Nirvana.
—Heart Sutra

In Hindu tradition, Nirvana signals the state of perfect quietude and freedom from *samsara,* the repeated rounds of rebirth. This sounds similar to what Antonio Machado utters poetically: "Deep peace to our bones . . . it is final now. Sleep our untroubled and true dream." I harbor no quarrel whatsoever with *nirvana*; sign me up!

(11) Continuing Manifestations

When we lose someone we love, we should remember that the person has not become nothing. Something cannot become nothing, and nothing cannot become something. They have taken on another form. That form may be a cloud, a child, or the breeze.

We can see our loved one in everything . . . in continuing manifestations.
—Thich Nhat Hanh

In my more numinous moments, I readily experience the presence of the deceased in daily sentiments and sensations. And as rapidly as our individual lights go out, they may be subsumed in the ongoing blaze of a fathomless universe. The peculiar flame of each of us may glisten forth in the sun, in our descendants, in an unfinished social cause, and in the stars. Our sparkle, even when no longer bearing our name, may shine on. I trustingly assert that post-dead reality can arrive in evolving forms, fresh energy, and unusual gifts: "continuing manifestations."

Hanh often employs the charming phrase: "wonderful becoming" which reminds me of the literal translation of *Yahweh* and certainly reflects the Unitarian Universalist marriage of *semper reformanda* and "everlasting love."

(12) Hoping for a Peep Hole

Lest this segment grow cumbersome, here's a playful thought from a dear colleague's mother, phrased shortly before her death:

> *When your world dies around you, you know it's time to go. You just get tired, but I hope there is a peep hole up here in heaven to be able to spy on my family and friends!*

How can one argue with this dying wish? It's a genial way of extending our own peculiar life-drama, a wish few of us would spurn.

Naturally, lots of "what-if's" kick in: what if my personal consciousness dies when I die; what if my destination is down below rather than up above; what if spying is deemed illegal or off-limits in either realm; and what if family or friends don't want me or anyone else (dead or alive!) snooping on them? And face it, there will likely be an in-law or out-law who just wishes I would shut the peep up!

XXII. *How do I hope to be remembered? What might I deem my legacy to be?*

Be a good ancestor, stand for something bigger than yourself, and add value to the Earth during your sojourn.
—Marian Wright Edelman

The Hebrew phrase for dying translates thusly: "being gathered unto one's people." Most of us yearn, upon death, to be gathered unto our people: our partners, families, friends, and faith community. We yearn to be remembered. That's the pertinence and power of having a memorial service in our own honor. For the opposite of being remembered isn't merely being forgotten but symbolically being dis-membered, torn asunder, cut off, and vanished.

How will we be remembered after we die? We're going to be dead far longer than we've been alive, so some remembrance of our personhood seems important. In our workshops, we engage in four "legacy" exercises (when time allows) as follow-up to our earlier Life-Review: (1) Composing an ethical will; (2) Organizing things in a Memorabilia Room; (3) Laying in notes for our own obituary notice as well as our Memorial Service eulogy; and (4) Crafting a deathbed poem or farewell letter.

First, an ethical will.

Patriarch Isaac, recognizing his days are numbered, calls his first born to him. He charges Esau, "so that I may give you my blessings before I die."
—Genesis 27

If a person leaves behind no one who remembers our values and character, if we are forgotten, we die a second death.
—Rabbi Harold Kushner

Parenting tasks are awesome, and our tenure may even "seem" forever, but, sooner or later, we die. Fathers and mothers suffer an unnecessary "second death," if we fail to transmit our ideals and visions to our children. Inability to pass on ethical and spiritual wisdom is a common familial plight. As a professional who does grief counseling, I'm oft-disturbed by the amount of unfinished business at the time of death, especially among parents and children.

I wrote my first book *Generation to Generation: Passing along the Good Life to Your Children* in 1986 as an attempt, while living, to share love-letters with our four children, intrepidly bequeathing some of my deepest concerns and hopes for them. I was making out what the Jewish culture calls an "ethical will." When you're dying, you are rarely in the best condition to illuminate your soul. There is also the likelihood that your grieving family or friends will be too shaky to hear what you might struggle to say.

So, I penned one in the prime of life and encourage *Mindful Dying* workshop participants to consider doing likewise. Composing an ethical will is an integral contribution toward *Making Peace with our Own Death*. I wrote 52 letters, one per week, but in our workshop I recommend a page-long epistle, deftly composed, then thereafter preferably shared with one child at a time, before graciously turning our brood loose to live the lives they will personify on their own. If you have more than one child, you may wish to customize each letter.

Archbishop Oscar Arnulfo Romero spoke out against the heinous social injustices in his homeland of El Salvador and was murdered in 1980. He offers a humbling reminder: "We are workers not master builders, ministers not messiahs. We are prophets of a future not our own." To be sure, we will not be around for the full lifetimes of the descendants to whom we're leaving our ethical wills. But we are suckling unknown tomorrows. Life does not end with our end. We keep on mattering. We are waves in an ongoing ocean, branches on the Tree of Life, and influencers of generations to come. We can always be a good ancestor.

The second activity is using a file cabinet, special closet, or entire room to store photos, articles, certificates, journals, and artifacts for family to peruse when we're dead. Carolyn and I have been doing this in rigorous fashion, filling a tiny bedroom where one of our children used to bunk, then a grandchild, and now it's a storage facility for valued memorabilia. We call it our *Room of Memories*.

We've found the process to be both invigorating and cathartic as we sort through remembrances of our individual and communal histories. If you're in a partnership, you should allow separate cabinets for each person. Additionally, as your life progresses toward death, it's prudent to keep re-examining your farewell materials.

Yet questions needle away. Will anyone choose to rake through this stuff? How much of real worth is contained in that room? How long will our keepsakes stay intact? In short, don't be too self-conscious about what you've earned or saved. Stephen Cushman jots an antidote to our overweening hunger for legacy:

The sky has never won a prize.
The clouds have no careers.
The rainbow doesn't say "my work."

The third exercise, during this segment, is the invitation for participants to rough out the story of our life for a newspaper Obituary Notice upon our death. This should include biographical data and salient life-events as well as depicting the core of what our existence epitomized. Achievements, relationships, challenges, even setbacks, are referenced.

What makes each of us an absolutely unique human being is the goal of this tribute? A page worth will suffice for the parameters of our *Mindful Dying* workshop and will furnish indispensable content for a lengthier Biographical Tribute delivered at your service. I have amassed in the *Green Book* an overload of fodder for my own tribute, which will need to be trimmed by both family and officiant in planning for my memorial service.

Obviously, testifiers, at the time of our memorial tribute, may not fully follow our lead, plus we're not around to make last minute amendments or to assist them. But my rationale holds: when you put down in print what you consider to be weighty about your own life and pass said notes on to family and/or friends, they'll, at least, know who you roughly thought you were. Everybody benefits from maximum truth-sharing before we die.

Finally, I invite participants/readers to consider crafting a "death poem"—the genre of poetry that developed in the literary traditions of East Asian cultures, most prominently in Japan (called a *jisei* or farewell poem). These verses classically present last minute, personal observations upon life.

Here's a *jisei* by Kozan Ichikyo, Zen monk, composed in 1360:
Empty-handed I entered the world
Barefoot I leave it.
My coming, my going—

Two simple happenings
That got entangled.

A contemporary version of a *jisei* is called "As I Lay Dying"—a dispatch written to your family and loved ones, offering your final thoughts and feelings. In workshops, this would again comprise no more than a page, which you can amplify, later on.

XXIII. *What are some specific plans for my memorial service— focusing on questions such as where, who, when, and what?*

Occasionally, UU's hold their own "memorial service" while they're still alive. This delivers one clear advantage: you will not only be able to compose what you wish to say out loud to loved ones, but also the favor can be returned. In short, you'll be present for your personalized death-celebration. Everything live and in Technicolor!

This won't be my plan, but I can envision holding a party on a specific birthday as I draw nearer my death, wherein we all might get a chance to commemorate our deeply cherished connections. Maybe there could also be a memorabilia table with photos and the like, even some video remembrances. Of course, at mine, there would be oodles of group singing which I would be fortunate to lead.

There are some folks in my workshops who decline having a memorial service, because they feel unworthy, estranged from family, utterly alone, or whatever. In workshops, I try to persuade participants to hold some sort of celebration, however modest or minimal, because I feel everyone deserves to be memorialized. But the verdict remains theirs.

I find that our Unitarian Universalist memorial services reveal more about our brand of religion than any other single event, ritual, or passage. At their finest, our services are truthful and loving. We aspire to honor each never-before and never-again dead person rather than focusing upon generalized and abstract doctrines. And our content (particularly, when the dead person has pre-recorded their own thoughts!) invariably resembles the idiosyncratic story and singular wishes of the deceased.

Our services are equally for both the grieving and the dead. The fibs and fabrications are negligible, and the event is festive and triumphant. Even memorials for still-borns or tragic, premature deaths such as children or *Aids* victims—as anguishing as they are—remain honest and honorable, individualized and comforting. In summation, our memorials are ushering every last soul into the company of "everlasting love."

Pause with me for a moment, as I envisage the origins of memorial services. This is not documented history but rather a morsel of pure fantasy. I've often pondered how we ministers ever got the job, in the first place, of burying our fellow kin. I mean: why us?

So, imagine professional assignments being dispensed, with farmers and pharmacists, tailors and teachers, welders and shamans all lined up and waiting to receive specific orders. And when it came time to ascribe funerals, I picture that the job-dispenser, whoever that might have been, turned to clergy in the crowd, and declared: "Okay, let's see; why don't the reverends—who are endlessly brooding over life-and-death matters—assume the responsibility of working with morticians and coordinating memorial celebrations? To be sure, pastors probably don't know how to do this job any better than the rest of us, since we're all *virgins* when it comes to death, but it just seems proper and fitting for you folks to take the lead: given your fascination with metaphysical affairs. So, give it a try, and check back with our vocational center, if you need any help!"

Well, centuries later, ministers continue to officiate during last rites: mingling scripture and melody, prayers and groans, tributes and silence, with a heart full of anxiety and a handy supply of dirt nearby. Clearly, it's both a sizable drain and a profound blessing to commemorate the dead, for every occasion constitutes a peculiar and precious passage. Remembering a fellow-traveler with truth and trembling is one of the greatest privileges any human being can ever claim. And wouldn't you know it: over time, memorials have become my favorite sacrament, because tears of gratitude, sadness, and remembrance are drawn and poured forth from such a mysterious and wondrous well.

Let's take a deep breath; then we'll move ahead.

Before we address specific plans for memorial services, here are some more *Green Book* tips. I apologize for the profuse details, but as they rightly say: "God dwells in the details!" And if the Almighty is impossible to find in the following minutiae, something of relevance to YOU is apt to be revealed there!

In my bulging *Green Book*, I have copiously (some might say compulsively) recorded my end-of-life wishes, plus everything about my personal heirlooms and belongings: clothing, books (blessedly, most have already been donated to the church library, colleagues, or family members), memorabilia, files, art pieces, magic and sports paraphernalia, musical materials and instruments, and special computer documents. I have pinpointed where they are located and, generally, to whom they might go. Despite trying to cover every nook and cranny of our house, including the garage, I've surely overlooked a few items. No worry, someone in the family will stumble upon them. Finders can be either keepers or tossers.

The *Green Book* also tells where all our legal, insurance, medical, and financial documents are to be found, in addition to the contact information of relatives and friends to notify when I die. Naturally, we have already pointed out where everything is to our son in San Diego, but in case Russ forgets, the information resides in the *Green Book*.

Carolyn and I also possess files of professional "papers" for family and friends to peruse, if desired, in the archives room at First UU Church of San Diego.

Additionally, issues such as memorial society preference, bodily disposition, memorial service contacts, the desired minister, and location of the service are all to be answered beforehand by each of us. Key point: make sure that all of your pre-death plans are shared with loved ones as well as the likely officiant at your chosen Church or memorial site.

Although I have been the primary crafter of the *Green Book*, discoverable therein are information and wishes for both Carolyn and myself. If I die before Carolyn, she will be the lead person processing and deciding about everything—and vice-versa.

I wind-up the *Green Book* with this paragraph:

As you beloveds know, there will be money and material items as well passed on to you, our children and grandchildren, but, most of all, we hope you will cherish the memories we shared and the meanings we created together. In the long run, that is what will sustain our souls. Our family connections are more important than any collections. We aspire to live on in and through our imperfect love. Love trumps all!

Okay, onward to specifics of our Memorial Services.

My following suggestions concerning Memorial Service plans are plainly to be modified by each *Mindful Dying* workshop individual. And remember, during a single session of the workshop, there will be only enough time for making initial notes. The workshop is but a jumpstart!

Here are principle matters, in no particular order, to address:

- Where, if at all, will my Obituary Notice (the beginning components of which I have already composed during the workshop) and announcement of my service be printed and/or publicized? And now, via e-mail lists and the like, survivors can spread the word of my death, both wisely and widely.

  Then there are questions regarding the particulars of my actual Memorial Service:

- What are my musical selections, classical and/ or popular, choral or instrumental? Do I have soloists and instrumentalists in mind and what hymns/songs might the congregation sing during the memorial?

- Who are the people (family and/or friends) whom I would like to speak?

  Three reminders: first, if possible, inform presenters

(including children and/or grandchildren) before you die why you chose them to speak on your behalf. Second, if any relative or friend turns you down, for whatever reason, they might write something instead that can be shared by the officiating minister. Third, if the service is held in a living room with an intimate gathering, personal tributes are appropriate. If the service is conducted in a sanctuary setting, open-mic sharing is discouraged. Personal and heartfelt notes can either be inscribed in the guestbook or disclosed later with the family.

Following the service, cart the guestbook over to the reception; so attendees, if desired, can spend more time composing comments. The guestbook, when expanded, turns into an album of remembrance for the family.

- What about the Chalice Lighting? Folks have found it deeply meaningful to have a younger family member be the lighter.
- What Call to Worship, responsive and other readings, and Benediction would I like shared? Our *Singing the Living Tradition* (Beacon Press, 1993) is a treasure-trove for texts, prayers, and musical selections. Plus, every minister has compiled a list of excellent readings; Carolyn and I certainly have.
- My Biographical Tribute constitutes the central element of the memorial celebration, to be supplemented, as desired, by the spoken contributions of family, officiant, and/or friends. Note previous comments on this process.
- What might a printed Order of Service look like: perhaps

my photo on the front, followed by birth and death dates; basic flow of the memorial service inside; and on the back cover—brief biographical notes, appropriate quotation, or important miscellany?

- What kind of floral and/or pictorial arrangement for the chancel area? Details finalized and provided by family, first for the sanctuary, and then everything is taken to the reception. Family disperses the flowers afterwards.

- When do I want the service to take place? Saturday or Sunday afternoons are optimal and accessible times for most people. Clearly, a date needs to be selected that will accommodate attendance of the maximum number of family members and close friends . . . from near and far.

- How about reception arrangements? Light food and drinks? Video (usually no more than 10 minutes) viewed perhaps during an announced break or shown continuously? Testimonial sharing might work during the reception, if emceed appropriately. I also find it sensible to have people mingle at the reception rather than have a formal receiving line.

- What about a Memorabilia Table? Such a table provides opportunity for attendees to view—at their own pace—photo albums, awards, personal artifacts, etc. In my case, copies of my authored books will be given freely as a take-away memento. You may wish to have similar items to dispense on your table.

- What about financial gifts? They can be given to an organization chosen by either the deceased and/or by attendees. Make sure the request is clear and known beforehand.

- What about ushers and guest book attendant? It is prudent

planning, once again, for you to make these designations before you die. Obviously, after you're gone, the family will render their own modifications.

Any and all other issues unaddressed here will be left to the co-planning of family, friends, and the minister. If the Officiant knows you fairly well, she/he/they will be able to "personalize" the entire content of the Memorial Service. This is an immeasurable blessing.

XXIV.   *During my final season how am I honoring the "Big Law?"*
        What more might I wish to say to and do for the Earth?

There's a really big law that we have to obey.
That law is respect.
We have to treat everything with respect.
The earth, the animals, the plants, the sky.
Everything.
—Catherine Attla

Catherine Attla (1927-2012), of the Nolcheena Clan of the Koyukon Athabascan nation, declares respect to be the big law of reality in a manner similar to the quintessential 7th principle of Unitarian Universalism: "respect for the interdependent web of all existence of which we are a part." Every moral and spiritual commitment proceeds from this touchstone, and all forms of respect are interlaced. As we gain abiding respect for water, soil, and sky, as well as plants and animals, we grow less likely to treat our fellow humans with disregard. Authentic respect is indivisibly relevant to creating greater justice across lines of color and identity, class and orientation, conviction and ability.

To phrase it biblically, we're members one with another, members of the same body. And where there is an ache or loss, distress or separation in one of the limbs, our whole-body shudders and rallies to restore equilibrium. Young or old, ministers or laity, animals or plants, we are intertwining limbs of the same cosmic corpus. We may not be able to save one another from affliction, but we can serve one another in the throes of it.

Stewarding the universe, the biosphere, and the ecosystem constitutes our foremost earthly mission. May we "live the interdependent web" wherever we're planted, in every zone of our living-and-dying. Note that our concluding Unitarian Universalist principle salutes the "web . . . of which we are a part." We humans are not seen as the final accomplishment but rather as an integral part. This places our humanity in proper perspective and is fully congruent with the position of Transcendentalist thinker, Elizabeth Peabody (1804-1894), who coined the word "egotheism"—the futile attempt of humans to deify ourselves.

We elders need to acknowledge, not just intellectually but viscerally, that we are related to and are a product of nature. We are of the loam. We are of the sea. We are of the air. Created of the same stuff, we are interdependent. We receive existence and sustenance from one another. We hang together; life exists in what Thich Nhat Hanh calls the state of "interbeing"—the connectedness of all phenomena.

We two-legged, ever-evolving lovers would be wise to start

with a readiness to *behold*. Not analyze or alter reality but simply behold it. Behold the lilies of the field. Behold the moon. Behold the raccoon. Behold the sunset. Behold even the tornado for we cannot wrest beauty from the whole. Everywhere we roam, we find loveliness mingled with the cruel and disturbing. And behold the rocks, for a brook without rocks has no song.

Then, during our final stretch, let us continue "to till and keep it," (the Garden of Eden)—to be caretakers of the planet. Life itself was deeded to human beings under the requirement that we prove obedient to the basic laws of the Creation and be responsible for its well-being. And don't forget: tilling means more than having a green thumb. Some of us don't own green thumbs, and we're hardly exempt from stewardship of the earth. We're all conscripted as planetary servants.

Respectful creatures behold, till, and then employ the essential tools to cultivate the earth's elements. We need the tools of technology, the tools of ethics, the tools of economics, the tools of politics, and the tools of the religious spirit—born in wonder, filled with gratitude, and employed reverently. Each individual act of compassion for the natural world, each measure of conservation, each decision against dirtying the air, land, or water . . . these gifts honor "the big law." Our planet will presumably survive, no matter what we earthlings do or fail to do, because the cosmos knows how to heal itself. Nonetheless, we humans can leave no greater legacy, after our death, than having handled the earth and all its inhabitants with exceeding care and tenderness.

Carolyn and I were blessed to spend every Wednesday (our day-off) with our last San Diego grandchild, Owen. We knew our days together were numbered, since when Owen reached school age, he would trundle off to class on Wednesdays. As Owen slyly put it, "Grandma and Grandpa, for now you have me!" One Wednesday, Owen, our theologian-in-training, popped up with an imponderable query, as only children are wont to do: "Grandma, does the earth talk?" And Carolyn shrewdly retorted: "Well, what do you think, sweetie?" "I think it does; when we hurt the Earth, it sneezes and when we're good to it, it's happy and smiles."

Owen's wisdom prevails: in becoming ever-evolving lovers of Earth, our farewell job is igniting more smiles than sneezes. May we live and die, as the Native Americans say, being honorable "earth-holders."

During the final session of our *Mindful Dying* workshop series, I invite participants to compose a spiritual manifesto to the cosmos. A page in length, I encourage workshop attendees to compile a modest list of abiding hopes for the future of our beloved universe. We emerged from the Earth and return unto it. We owe it our undying praise and prayerful wishes.

As able, I also invite participants/readers to take a saunter, meandering through a backyard garden or nearby park, beholding every beast of the field and outdoor sprig, in full recognition that we cradle the same fate as these sacred kin. The Japanese call this practice *shinrin-yoku* or "forest-bathing." It is our time to shower thanks upon forests that make our atmosphere more breathable. They are under dire threat; so are we. May this jaunt soak in gratitude, as we appreciate the plants and animals who have taken good care of *us* during the course of our respective journeys.

Home-stretchers would do well to internalize the ancient Celtic imagination that welcomed nature, divinity, and human existence as equal partners in one unified cosmos, every bit of it rampant with soul. Animals and shrubbery are our relations. Wells are sacred sites. Rivers and streams are the outpouring of earth's emotionality. Is it any wonder that Unitarian Universalists finally came to our senses, resonated with our ancestors, and celebrated earth-based spirituality as one of our sacred sources?

This final homage proclaims, loud and clear, our spiritual aspirations for an Earth that we will no longer be enjoying in our present physical form. It is beautifully recapped in Dag Hammarskjöld's inspirational decree: "For all that has been—Thanks; for all that shall be—Yes!"

EPILOGUE

Returning to the
"Everlasting Love of God"

To get over deathophobia, we must learn to love the end.
—Stephen Jenkinson

She died happy. She was a Universalist.
—Drusilla Cummins

Dying is surrender to the earth and God's embrace.
—Pierre Teilhard de Chardin

True religion is surrender.
—Mohammed

Soon enough, we elders and crones will be done with our human living and off to our human dying. But, here and now, we abide, finishing life fully and facing death boldly . . . staying awake and making sufficient peace until our final gasp. Along with cultural activist, Jenkinson (1954-), my prayerful wish would be not merely to bear, but also to love, my one and only earthly end. Will my aspiration become my accomplishment? Who knows? I'm not there yet. However, I do fancy going out like sister Drusilla: *happy*.

Then there's the perceptive phrase of Teilhard (1881-1955), French philosopher and Jesuit priest. Truly, you and I are helpless both at moment of birth and at moment of death. Our final assignment is to surrender to the earth and to God, the mysteries that fashioned us. The word surrender is derived from "render" which means to give back. Our very existence is a pure and precious gift. We don't own our "being;" we can't even hang on to it. We've been blessed to possess it for a stretch. Our dying act is tenderly returning our body to its Source.

And here's my exegesis of the Prophet Mohammed's (571-632 A.D.) *four* crucial words: "True religion is surrender." Pretty much everything has been felt, thought, preached, and done in the name of religion—rapture, brutality, compassion, and subservience. Yet, religion, at its truest, means: shedding physicality, releasing outcomes, canning biases, abandoning dreams, even posthumous hopes and submitting our all . . . back, back, back to an ever-expanding, benevolent Cosmos. Surrendering, ah surrendering.

In my adolescence, I clung to God in a way that didn't do justice to either of us. Then I rebelled (even while studying in seminary, naturally, during the "God is Dead!" epoch) and retreated, early in my ministry, into a comfortable religious humanism and relative self-sufficiency. But I've kept evolving. *Semper reformanda.* Now, preparing to face death head-on, I stand ready and willing to relinquish my being to the Creation that birthed me, has nurtured and stretched me ever since, and will cradle me when I die.

In yielding to the Eternal Spirit, submission isn't required, but trust is. Indeed, the Hebrew word for faith, *bitachon*, essentially means trust which constitutes the union of some data, gamble, buoyancy, grace, risk, and ample release. I recall, as I contemplate my own death, the poetic phrase of Philip Booth:

Lie gently and wide to the light-year stars.
Lie back and the sea will hold you.

Booth is pointing to what classic Christianity has called the loving arms of Jesus or what our Universalist faith implies when it encourages us to "rest assured," confident that all living creatures will finally dwell in the embrace of God. This unshakeable trust makes love achievable and death endurable.

As a senior in the midst of taking a slew of final exams, I confess to being a tight-fisted, high-control guy. Trust isn't normally my optimal condition. Yet I'm shifting glacially, surrendering pieces and moments of control, conceit, and coveting. I'm lightening my load and "hallowing my diminishments" as Teilhard deftly expresses.

I'm detaching some of my ego needs and cleaving to less and less and less as I trek toward what Irish poet and priest John O'Donohue (1956-2008) called "the house of eternal belonging." Right now, in my loft-office, I've taken a breather from writing, and I'm crooning one of my much-loved African-American spirituals, "I'm On My Way." And as the song invites: I'm asking surrounding sisters and brothers to come go with me; but if they choose not to, "I'll go anyhow . . . "

In this same vein, at a recent *Unitarian Universalist Retired Ministers and Partners Association* retreat, I performed a solitary exercise for achieving deeper peace with my own death. Three consecutive early mornings, I walked a bucolic, stone-ridden labyrinth amid the placid Arizona foothills. As I strode meditatively, I pondered three spiritual imperatives of my farewell process: gratefully letting go, graciously letting be, and gently letting come.

For me, there's no better mode of settling in the present moment than performing a modest *gassho*, a bowing ritual of Eastern origin. My hands are pressed together in front of the chest and used as a greeting of reverence and caring. I employ a *gassho* in an inconspicuous manner, mainly to redirect my own self to the eternal *now*. A *gassho* means paying respectful attention to all that arises. In bowing, we let our head drop, hold our ego in check, and unseal our heart. Taoism reminds us that in a storm, the bamboo tree that can bend and bow with the wind will survive. Hence, in my daily flow, I aspire to take four basic bows:

I bow to the needs and purposes of the universe.
I bow to the betterment of our world community.
I bow to the welfare of every living being I greet.
I bow to my own self-enhancement.

A *gassho* is gratitude in movement. I began and ended this labyrinth ritual with a full-blown, languorous *gassho*: bowing to the entirety of my life-sweep.

Letting go: I acknowledged ownership of the hurts and hallelujahs, hassles and hopes of my past. I prayed to reach harmony with who I was and wasn't, then unfetter the bulk of my yesteryear.

Letting be: I swore to take up residence in the eternal now.

Letting come: I vowed to welcome my unknown tomorrows.

I walked the labyrinth in the same manner that I daily chant and meditate: with my hands cupped and outstretched.

And I remembered: we are born with our fists clenched as babies, but when we arrive at death's door, our hands are flung open. During the intervening days and nights, we're summoned progressively to unclench our fists and extend our hands in reverence toward every object and living entity that crosses our path: accepting the outlier, massaging the maimed, and fostering genuine intimacy. Then, upon death, wide open of hand and heart, we dissolve, we melt, we return to "everlasting love."

Today, July 20, 2020, as I am inching toward a completed draft of *Making Peace with Our Own Death*, Carolyn and I learned about the death of the Rev. Dr. Oliver Eugene Pickett at the age of 94. Gene was our dear friend and esteemed mentor who co-chaired Carolyn's run for the UUA presidency from 1991-1993 and about whom I composed a biography: *O. Eugene Pickett—Borne on a Wintry Wind* (Skinner House, 1996).

Pickett served as President of the UUA (1979-1985) and guided our movement from a period of decline to an era of growth. He was a supremely collaborative leader who combined imagination and activism. Gene brought the best out in people as well as served purposes and produced results larger than his own identity. He embodied religious authority in the fullest sense of the Latin verb *augere*, meaning "to cause to grow," to augment that which already is.

Furthermore, rarely did a sermon or a talk delivered by Pickett during his presidential years fail to allude to the centrality and power of facing our human mortality. His very first General Assembly address in 1979 was no exception. He staunchly declared:

Afraid that we would find our doctrines wanting, we have fled from the face of death. And any faith which cannot step boldly, trembling, up to death will be a shrinking faith . . .

Call it grace, mystery, or possibility but our Unitarian Universalist faith must meet the dying with lips shaping just one word—an eternal, immutable "Yes!"

Amen!

Mindful Dying Workshop

It's important that when we come to die,
we have nothing to do but to die.
—Charles Hode

DETAILS OF THE MINDFUL DYING WORKSHOP

Conscious aging and mindful dying are two interlinking workshops that I have been conducting at Unitarian Universalist congregations in recent years. Undoubtedly, what the influx of younger ministerial colleagues need from elder pastors is the willingness to take the lead on these topics. And that's what I'm doing. Understandably, as a good faith home-stretcher, I'm also shepherding these seminars for the nourishment of my own soul.

What follows are the basic logistics and format for my typical four-session *Mindful Dying* series. There is an abundance of material in this book from which such workshops can be shaped, but for purposes of an abbreviated seminar sequence, I have trimmed appropriately. As a program leader, I presume you will adapt what follows based upon your own needs and desires.

Description
Title: *Mindful Dying—Preparing for Our Own Farewell*

Being bona fide heretics ("choice-makers"), we Unitarian Universalists are challenged to address the social and spiritual aspects of our own departures before our death knells are sounded.

During these supportive sessions, we will exchange notes on pressing fears and other complex emotions as well as desired physical and spiritual elements of a "good death." Participants will compose a life-review and begin mapping out wants and plans for our own memorial services. We will address "how do we wish to be remembered?" and explore multiple views on "what happens to us after we die?"

Two Notes:
First, the above blurb should be publicized, weeks ahead, then repeatedly, in all modes of parish communication.

Second, since I'm not in current settlement, before conducting each workshop, I always request the endorsement of the in-resident pastor and/or religious education professional.

I directly coordinate with whoever may be overseeing adult programs in the congregation. In fact, it might be wise, when possible, to co-lead the class with either program staff or with a lay-person from said parish.

Participation

Anyone who wishes to attend may do so. Seniors are specifically encouraged to participate, but any adult may do so, both for their own edification as well as for the opportunity to companion an aging family member or friend. I've entertained all ages and combinations. This workshop is geared to members and friends, but like-minded associates beyond your congregation are certainly welcome to partake. That has happened as well.

I recommend pre-registration, because knowing numbers beforehand helps the leader prepare for quantity of materials. While I prefer 20 or so registrants, I've had upwards of 40. If the room is too small, simply find another location. If this procedure doesn't suit you, then you may wish to schedule two smaller sessions, months apart.

Schedule

Since evenings are more difficult for seniors to manage, I generally book Saturday mornings from 9 a.m.-Noon, although weekday mornings function as well. I have focused upon four sessions, because all generations in today's world rarely commit to more than four. While attendance at every session is desirable, it is not mandatory. Participants are often sick or away and unable to attend.

There is no need to furnish food or even snacks; it complicates matters. I would rather be personally accessible to greet and talk with participants, from start to finish, than worrying about food supply and setup. My preference may not be yours! However, providing water bottles has worked well.

Location

I like to hold *Mindful Dying* in a place of sacredness in the congregation, if possible. For example, at First UU Church, I held it in our chapel (capacity of 50 seats) which was a cozy and comfortable room for the 40+ who attended. When we broke into dyads, participants could go outside or into another room for optimal intimacy and hearing. In short, find a room on your campus that has warmth, beauty, and appropriateness for such a workshop.

> **Note:**
> Often my series has spawned an ongoing support group co-led by the minister/religious educator and a lay leader. *Mindful Dying* workshops should become a meaningful staple in the program life of our Unitarian Universalist societies. The relevance of the theme is both timely and enduring.

Cost

I recommend the workshop be free of charge, unless the church program life needs reimbursement, and, in that case, it should be a "suggested donation." The leader/leaders, coming from within the community itself, are never paid. Only outside presenters are remunerated.

Set-Up

- Podium which the leader can use for formal sharing, although I roam as well
- Easel with butcher paper, marking pens, and tape (in case, you attach sheets on surrounding walls)
- Lavalier microphone, if needed; in any case, strongly urge participants and leader as well to project voices when contributing in large group
- Singing bowl used to demarcate program segments and call people back to the larger group
- A flaming chalice with matches and snuffer
- If group is 15-20 or fewer persons, I suggest being seated in a circle

Materials (provided)

- Small notebooks and writing utensils (usually obtainable from the RE department)
- Reproduced handouts such as the opening 7 aspirations, chants, questions, quotations, and bibliography
- Name tags for participants, to supplement those brought by members
- Books available for viewing, checking-out, and purchasing. At First Church we are fortunate to have a library with a robust section on *Death and Dying* resources, so I borrow these books for the duration of the series, as well as volumes from my own personal collection. Books can be loaned out for one session at a time. And when my book *Making Peace with Our Own Death* is published, it will be available for purchase. I will reference it early on and have copies sitting

on a table at the front of the room, along with the other library books.

Flow

I. Welcome

I personally begin each session with both a chant (note sheet) and one evocative quotation (note collection) as a participant is invited to light the flaming chalice. Clearly, each leader will sculpt each session as they choose.

II. Schedule

I post beforehand the schedule of each session on the easel board.

III. At the first session, if the group is under 15, I ask each participant to stand, as willing and able, and to share one major takeaway they are seeking. As the leader, I make a mental note or may write these "hopes" down on the butcher paper, even post them on the walls, for the duration of the series. Obviously, this protocol depends upon the group size.

At the beginning of each ensuing class, I ask if there are any personal issues or comments to share on Mindful Dying that bubbled up during the week. Short reflections.

IV. In the first session, I go over my 7 Mindful Dying Aspirations, engaging folks in group dialogue on each one. This process may take considerable time, but it warms participants up to the overall topic and each other, and it helps to establish common ground.

V. Establish group process guidelines (in the first session)
Samples: use I-language; don't speak twice until everyone who wishes to share has spoken; confidentiality (what is shared, stays in the room); the right to reticence (no one has to say anything out loud); and project our voices at all times. Of course, there are often other group guidelines that are suggested. Make this a fair but non-laborious process. Write them on the board and keep the sheets visible for every session. Further guidelines can always be added.

VI. Addressing Each Question
I begin with my own commentary. When I am speaking, I use a microphone, depending upon the acoustics of the room. However, in any case, always be cognizant of the fact that many of the participants will have hearing issues, including myself. Speak slowly and strongly.

After the leader's commentary, there are three succeeding stages:

(1) Individuals compose personal notes in response to each question.

(2) The group then breaks into dyads (partners who came together are understandably encouraged to match up), allowing plenty of time for back-and-forth sharing. If there happens to be an odd number of participants, try triads. However, I often meet up with one of the extra participants.

(3) We reconvene as a large group and entertain discussion. The time allotments given each question will vary, based upon the energy generated by the exchanges and upon the overall format plan of the leader.

Note:

Noticeably, there are far more questions available in the heart of this book. The leader may choose to add questions to each session, if time allows. More likely, the supplemental questions will be employed in the meetings of an ongoing support group.

Here are other suggestions for follow-up experiences in your parish.

First, you may choose to launch a book discussion group using one of the volumes on the bibliography list. Second, you may use passages from one of these books as a discussion starter in your support group. Third, you may employ one of the plentiful and provocative quotations as conversation fodder. In short, the resources in the Appendices can be utilized productively to sustain the momentum of parishioners in making greater peace with our own death and dying. Fourth, in some congregations the series has sparked an entire worship service on *Mindful Dying* with testimonies coming from participants and coordinated liturgically with the professional staff.

Two Notes:

First: Remember to have a 10-minute break about mid-way through every 3-hour class. At the first session, make sure that everyone knows where the restrooms are. Remember there may well be newcomers to your campus.

Second: During the break, I invariably stay in the room, in case participants wish to talk personally with me. I also come early, set up everything and greet arrivals, as well as remain around after each session for confidential conversation. This workshop is a highly emotional endeavor, and counseling support will prove invaluable.

Wrap-up (at each session)

(1) Ask if there are any closing comments folks would briefly like to make.

(2) If the group is small enough, you may wish to circle up and close with one of the chants as well as repeating together the chosen quotation on the board.

Otherwise, remain as a large group. The session closes as our flaming chalice is extinguished.

Ending (of the Entire Series)

Spend sufficient time allowing each person to check-out (not of life but of the series! ☺) by having them write down personal homework assignments they plan to address in the days ahead. One prime question for participants to explore repeatedly is: What practical matters and spiritual issues remain *unresolved* in my life regarding my dying and death?

> **Note:**
> In many of my workshops, as noted earlier, there has been a strong urge and need to re-configure as an ongoing support group.

Evaluation Sheet

Preferably taken home and filled out, mailed/brought back in, and signed, only if participants desire to do so.

- What were the strong points of this workshop?
- What important topics were missing?
- Would I recommend it to others?
- Would I sign up to participate in an ongoing support group here at First Parish?
- Here are additional materials and/or supportive resources that I would recommend for future classes.
- Are there other ways in which First Parish can support me in the days ahead in preparing for my own death? Are my end-of-life wishes on file? Do I desire pastoral counseling?

These evaluations should definitely be shared with the in-resident church staff for their professional knowledge and use.

7 MINDFUL DYING ASPIRATIONS

I. **Embrace the Reality**

A person asked the *roshi* if she might study with him. "Are you prepared to die?" "I didn't come here to die. I came here to learn Zen." Then the *roshi* replied: "If you are not willing to die, you are not ready to let go into life. Come back when you are ready."

Death is inevitable (100% fact), natural (fate of all living entities), and even desirable (intensifies our capacity and desire to live/love more fully right now).

II. **Die Daily**

"*To practice death is to practice freedom.*"
—Montaigne (1533-1592)

Shedding attachments (physical, emotional, relational, and spiritual) along the path prepares us to release everything when we cease breathing. Learning to die is learning to release our current holdings, opening afresh to every next moment without clinging . . . finally dissolving into the ocean of being.

III. **Live in Gratitude**

"*i thank You God for most this amazing day*"
—e. e. cummings

How are we showing appreciation and thankfulness during the remaining seasons of our earthly incarnation?

IV. **Exude Generosity**

Every day let us share or give away something: object, emotion, job, connection, and dream . . . ultimately, our very body.

How can we muster the energy and courage to live homeward-bound with a magnanimous and overflowing heart?

V. **Prepare for Our Own Farewell**
You only get one death. Live it.
—Bianca Nogrady

This process may prove arduous but, as Rilke said, "Love means holding to the difficult." There is no perfect or pure way to die; let us settle for dying with adequate grace and being wide-open to wonder. We all seek to experience a good, fitting death.

We stand ready and willing, during this workshop, to face our fears, regrets, anger, sadness, shortcomings, and losses as well as clarify our hopes and wishes about our own death—crafting our Life Review, epitaph, obit, and memorial service.

How can such preparation prove to be an enlightening and empowering endeavor for both ourselves and for our loved ones and friends?

VI. **Acknowledge that Dying and Death are Mysteries**
Leave the door open for the unknown, the door into the dark.
That's where the important things come from . . .
where you yourself came from, and where you will go.
—Rebecca Solnit

This is the time, at the outset of *Mindful Dying,* to recognize that among us there will be a plethora of viewpoints held and shared on this ticklish, complicated topic, so let us practice full acceptance of our diversity. After all, none of us in the room has finally died before.

VII. **Surrender Our Being**

During our homestretch we aspire to let the past go, let the present be, and let the future come. Our hope is, as Stephen Jenkinson urges, "to love the end!"

QUESTIONS FOR 4 SESSIONS

Session I

(1) What are your three favorite words or phrases to describe dying/death and why?

(2) In your daily life, how are you practicing death (saying goodbye to people, stuff, dreams, capacities, memories, etc.)? Give examples.

Session II

(1) What are your primary fears, regrets, and sadnesses regarding dying/death and how are you facing them?

(2) Compose your *Life-Review*, addressing turning points such as:
— defining/nourishing moments/bonds of your life, giving each a title and sentence or more.
— challenging/stressful issues of your life, assigning a simple lesson for how you have dealt with each.
— whom do you wish to ask for and/or deliver forgiveness?

(3) Are you ready to die tomorrow? If so, why? If not, what words and emotions might be shared, or actions accomplished in order to bring a greater sense of completion to your life?

(4) List some of the physical and spiritual elements that would constitute a "good/fitting death" for you—addressing

matters such as what, where, who (alone or accompanied), when, and how?

Session III

(1) What dies with you, when you die? What/who are you leaving behind? What/who will you miss most?

(2) What happens to you after you die? In sum, what is your theology/philosophy of post-death reality?

(3) How do you wish to be remembered? Compose your own personal six-word memoir. Then craft a short tribute (50 words or less) that captures the heart of who you've been and what you've stood for.

Session IV

(1) Craft an "Obituary Notice" and an outline for your "Biographical Tribute." Lay in beginning notes/plans for your memorial service, focusing upon questions such as location and time, officiant and participants, spoken and musical content of the celebration, including particulars of the aftermath?

(2) Script a page's worth of farewell words/tribute to our Earth?

(3) *Optional*: Gather together as group in a quiet and meditative state. Imagine you are dying now. What does it feel like? Share your responses in dyads, then, as a total group.

Making Peace with Our Own Death

QUOTATIONS ON DEATH AND DYING

Death is absolutely safe, like taking off a tight shoe.
Our goal is to die as consciously as possible.
—Ram Dass

Death will never die. Death is the pervasive root of the
Universe, always with you, always bringing new life.
—Karen Wyatt

Today is a good day to die; for all the things of
my life are present.
—Crazy Horse, Native American elder

Every coffin, asks us: "whither?"
—Robert Ingersoll

We can't cheat death but we can make it work
so hard that when it does take us,
it will have known a victory just as perfect as ours.
—Charles Bukowski

Death is our wedding with eternity.
—Rumi

If this were your last day, would you be satisfied?
—Lewis Mumford

I shall die, but that is all I shall do for death.
—Edna St. Vincent Millay

Death is but a transition from this life to another existence,
where there is no more pain and anguish.
Everything is bearable when there is love.
The only thing that lives forever is love.
—Elizabeth Kubler-Ross

If the dead be truly dead, why should they
be walking in my heart?
—Shoshone medicine healer

It's not that I'm afraid to die. I just don't want
to be there when it happens.
—Woody Allen

How do you suppose some people will spend Eternity when
they don't know how to spend the next half hour?
—Ralph Waldo Emerson

Thanks, thanks for everything; praise, praise, for it all.
—St. John of Chrysostom

Can you let go of your history and step into the mystery?
—Buddhist teaching

The end is not just the cessation of my life but the purpose
of my life as well, the purpose God intended in my creation.
That intent can never be fulfilled in a single lifetime but
only in what flows a lifetime, both here on earth and in my
return to that goodness by which we were born.
—Carl Scovel

Love doesn't die, people do; so when all that's left
of me is love, give me away.
—Anonymous

The great sea has set me in motion, set me adrift,
moving me like a weed in a river.
The sky and the strong wind have moved the spirit
inside me till I am carried away,
trembling with joy.
—Inuit Shaman Uvavnuk

Living while dying is our final human act . . . a divine art.
—Karen Speerstra

Growing older does not necessarily mean becoming wiser or kinder. Many die jealous, bitter, and angry. It's a choice.
—Gary Zukav

And so long as you haven't experienced this: to die and so to grow, you are only a troubled guest on the dark earth.
—Goethe

Life's goal is to give birth to oneself in the world before leaving it.
—Michel de M'Uzan

Why not go down . . . into the lake, consciously, like Beowulf. Don't die on the shore.
—David Whyte

I am and will be until I die—a self in evolution.
—George Sheehan

The way of death whispers in your ear: "There is only love."
—Karen Wyatt

Buddha meditated under a tree, was enlightened under a tree, and died lying down between two trees.
—Norman Fischer

The trees in a forest care for each other, sometimes even nourishing the stump of a felled tree for centuries after it was cut down by feeding it sugars and other nutrients, and so keeping it alive.
—Tim Flannery

Death comes as the one silence, the one that is blest by love, "the deepest buried love."
—Derek Walcott

Death is our friend precisely because it brings us into absolute and passionate presence with all that is here, that is natural, and that is love. Life always says Yes and No simultaneously. Death (I implore you to believe) is the true yea-sayer. It stands before eternity and says only: Yes.
—Rainer Maria Rilke

However, many more breaths are left me to breathe, to aspire and conspire, I know that with my final breath, I will be in the middle of learning yet another life lesson. That makes life all the more precious.
—Jane Bramadat

Life is pleasant. Death is peaceful. It's the transition that troubles me.
—Isaac Asimov

Let come what comes, let go what goes. See what remains.
—Ramana Maharshi

On the day when death will knock at thy door,
what wilt thou offer death?
I will set before my guest the full vessel of my life.
I will never let death go with empty hands.
—Rabindranath Tagore

There is no cure for birth and death, save to enjoy the interval.
—George Santayana

She whom we love and lose is no longer where she was
before. She is now wherever we are.
—St. John Chrysostom

It is usually proclaimed that birth, aging, and death are
suffering. If we don't grasp (tanha), they are not suffering;
they are only bodily changes.
—Ajahn Buddhadasa

My life is poured out like water,
and all my bones are out of joint.
My heart is like wax, melting within me.
My strength has dried up like sunbaked clay.
My tongue sticks to the roof of my mouth.
You have laid me in the dust and left me for dead.
—Psalm 22:14-15

A Zen student queried her master as to what happens after
death. The master smiled and said, "I do not know."
"How can that be? You are a Zen master."
"Yes, but I am not a dead Zen master!"

As my wife lies dying, I fully realize that love doesn't
eliminate, but simply neutralizes, the pain.
—Erving Polster

To die "isagi-yoku" is one of the aspirations of the
Japanese heart. It means dying bravely,
with a clear conscience, leaving no regrets . . .
—Daisetz T. Suzuki

This late August day—
together on the same branch
dead leaves and live ones.
—Gary Thorp

Who wields a poem larger than the grave? Love.
—e. e. cummings

Let it come as it will, and don't be afraid.
God does not leave us comfortless,
so let evening come.
—Jane Kenyon

And the dust returns to the earth as it was,
And the spirit returns to God who gave it.
—Ecclesiastes 12:7

There is no right way to die, no perfect personality
that we have to emulate. All we can do is be who
we are and allow death to take us as it will.
—Rodney Smith

All will be well. All will be well.
Every manner of thing will be well.
—Mother Julian of Norwich (1342-1416)

Let's face it; we will be intimate with death at least once.
—Kathy Kortes-Miller

What I know when we die is that
the song once sung cannot be unsung.
And the life once lived cannot be unlived,
a life once loved cannot be unloved.
—Kenneth Collier

All the universe has come from love and
unto love all things return.
—Taittiriya Upanishad

Death whispers in my ear; Live! I'm coming!
—Tacitus, Roman historian and poet

When people are dying, only two things matter. They just
want to know: Was I loved and did I love well?
Love: that's all that really matters.
—Frank Ostaseski

And God exhaled. When do we exhale? Perhaps, like God,
we exhale, when we feel certain that our
good and necessary work is done.
—Wayne Muller

At the deepest heart of your life, in your soul, there is no fear of death. It will change you, and change you beyond recognition to those you leave behind, but death cannot disassemble you.
—John O'Donohue

Afraid of dying, Emperor Su Tsung of the Tang dynasty asked the great teacher Chung Hui, "After you die, what you will need?" And I asked myself the same question. My mind said, "Nothing." My heart uttered, "Love."
—Mark Nepo

You are not dead yet, it's not too late to open your depths by plunging into them and drinking in the life that reveals itself quietly there.
—Rainer Maria Rilke

I can't die now; I'm booked.
—George Burns

On the morning the poet William Stafford died (1993) he wrote: *Be ready for what God sends!*

Every death is like the burning of a library.
—Alex Haley

We spend our whole lives trying to stop death. Eating,
inventing, loving, praying, fighting, killing. But what do
we really know about death? Just that nobody comes back.
But there comes a point in life, a moment, when your mind
outlives its desires. Maybe death is a gift.
—David Gale

Each person's life can be summed up in one sentence,
and it should be one that has an active verb.
—Clare Booth Luce

Of all footprints . . .
that of the elephant is supreme;
of all mindfulness meditations . . .
that on death is supreme.
—Buddhist sutra

Death is not the problem. Fear is.
And fear is something we create.
—Julia Assante

I wish I understood the beauty in falling leaves.
To whom are we beautiful as we're going?
—David Ignatow

The more you are able to become present in the moment;
the more you can feel like, if death happened now,
it would be OK. I have led the best life I can.
—Mirabai Bush

With every passing day,
we create the kind of death we will have.
—Sallie Tisdale

Rehearse death. To say this is to tell a person
to rehearse their freedom.
—Seneca (4 BC-AD 65),
Hispano-Roman Stoic philosopher and statesman

What if, as death approached, you found there was, after
all, nothing to be frightened of? What if we began to feel
contentedly part of the great cycle of nature
(please, take my carbon atoms)?
—Julian Barnes

Grant that my last hour might be my best hour.
—English Book of Hours

When the eye of the body is shut by death,
the eye of the soul opens to a far brighter light.
—The Egyptian Book of the Dead

Spiritual care is not an optional extra for the dying.
—Cicely Saunders

In hospice, they talk about the 5 things you should say to a dying loved one: thank you, I love you, please forgive me, I forgive you, and goodbye. The good news is that you can start saying the first four anytime.
—Katy Butler

In the end these things matter most:
How well did you love?
How fully did you live?
How deeply did you let go?
—Buddha

I am making my last effort to return
that which is divine in me to that
which is divine in the universe.
—Plotinus (205-270 C.E.)

CHANTS

I. Gathered here in the mystery of the hour.   **Christian**
Gathered here in one strong body.
Gathered here in the struggle and the power.
Spirit, draw near.

II. I am a circle, I am healing you.   **Native American**
You are a circle, you are healing me.
Unite us, make us one.
Unite us, make us one.

III. There is a love holding me/us.   **Unitarian Universalist**
There is a love holding all that I/we love.
There is a love holding all.
I/We rest in this love.

IV. Om Nama Shiva…   **Hindu**
   Om nama shiva…
      Om nama shiva…
         Shiva om nama.

V. May I be filled with loving kindness.   **Buddhist**
    May I be well.
    May I be filled with loving kindness.
    May I be well.
    May I be peaceful and at ease. May I be whole.

    Second time: replace each "I" with "you."
    Third time: replace each "I" with "we."

VI. Return again, return again   **Jewish**
    Return to the home of your soul. (repeat)

    Return to who you are, return to what you are, return to
    where you are…born and reborn again.

Making Peace with Our Own Death

Bibliography

This bibliography comprises a sampling of both classic and offbeat books, secular and religious, oldies and newbies. All are trackable on the Internet.

(1)   Barnes, Julian. *Nothing to Be Frightened Of.* New York: Vintage Books, 2009.

(2)   Becker, Ernest. *The Denial of Death.* New York: The Free Press, 1973.

(3)   Butler, Katy. *The Art of Dying Well: A Practical Guide to a Good End of Life.* New York: Scribner, 2019.

(4)   Copeland, Cyrus, M. editor. *Farewell, Godspeed: The Greatest Eulogies of Our Time.* New York: Harmony Books, 2003.

(5)   Dass, Ram and Bush, Mirabai. *Walking Each Other Home: Conversations on Loving and Dying.* Boulder, CO: Sounds True, 2018.

(6)   Gawande, Atul. *Being Mortal: Illness, Medicine, and What Matters in the End.* New York: Holt and Company, 2014.

(7)   Grollman, Earl. *When Your Loved One Has Died.* Boston: Beacon Press, 1980.

(8)   Halifax, Joan. *Being with Dying: Cultivating Compassion and Fearlessness in the Presence of Death.* Boston: Shambhala, 2009.

(9)   Hanh, Thich Nhat. *No Death, No Fear: Comforting Wisdom for Life.* New York: Riverhead Books, 2002.

(10)   Hitchens, Christopher. *Mortality.* New York: Grand Central Publishing, 2012.

(11)   Jenkinson, Stephen. *Die Wise: A Manifesto for Sanity and Soul.* Berkeley: North Atlantic Books, 2015.

Bibliography

(12)   Kalanithi, Paul. *When Breath Becomes Air*. New York: Random House, 2016.

(13)   Kapleau, Philip. *The Zen of Living and Dying*. Boston: Shambhala Publications, 1987.

(14)   Kortes-Miller, Dr. Kathy. *Talking About Death Won't Kill You: The Essential Guide to End-of-Life Conversations*. Toronto: ECW Press, 2018.

(15)   Kubler-Ross, Elizabeth. *Questions and Answers on Death and Dying*. New York: Collier Books, 1974.

(16)   Leder, Steve. *The Beauty of What Remains*. New York: Avery, 2021.

(17)   Levine, Stephen. *Healing into Life and Death*. New York: Anchor Books, 1987.

(18)   Lief, Judith L. *Making Friends with Death: A Buddhist Guide to Encountering Mortality*. Boulder: Shambhala, 2001.

(19)   Ostaseski, Frank. *The Five Invitations: Discovering What Death Can Teach Us about Living Fully*. New York: Flatiron Books, 2017.

(20)   Shaffer, Nancy. *While Still There is Light: Writings from a Minister Facing Death*. Boston: Skinner House Books, 2013.

(21)   Singh, Kathleen Dowling. *The Grace in Dying: How We Are Transformed Spiritually as We Die*. New York: Harpers One, 2000.

(22)   Smith, Rodney. *Lessons from the Dying*. Boston: Wisdom Publications, 2015.

(23)   Speerstra, Karen and Anderson, Herbert. *The Divine Art of Dying: How to Live Well While Dying*. Published by DivineArtsMedia.com, 2014.

(24)   Tisdale, Sallie. *Advice for Future Corpses: A Practical Perspective on Death and Dying*. New York: Touchstone, 2018.

About Tom Owen-Towle

The Rev. Dr. Tom Owen-Towle has been a parish minister since 1967 and is the author of two dozen books on personal relationships and spiritual growth. Tom and his life-partner, the Rev. Dr. Carolyn Sheets Owen-Towle, are the active parents of four children, seven grandchildren, and one great-grandchild. Tom is a guitarist, parlor magician, and currently sings with seniors, mentors children and youth, and volunteers with San Diego's homeless. Owen-Towle is a national leader who continues to conduct workshops and retreats on the core themes of his books.

FLAMING CHALICE PRESS publishes books on Unitarian Universalism, personal relationships, and spiritual growth. You can order copies of *Making Peace with Our Own Death* on www.amazon.com. If you would like to contact Tom Owen-Towle, you may reach him through one of the following ways:

Tom Owen-Towle
3303 Second Avenue
San Diego, CA 92103
Tel: (619) 933-1121
Email: uutom@cox.net
Web: www.tomo-t.com

Made in the USA
Monee, IL
14 June 2023

35818998R10142